ANCIENT NEAR EAST

THE BASICS

Ancient Near East: The Basics surveys the history of the ancient Middle East from the invention of writing to Alexander the Great's conquest. The book introduces both the physical and the intellectual environment of those times, the struggles of state-building and empire construction, and the dissent from those efforts. Topics covered include:

- What do we mean when we talk about the Ancient Near East?
- The rise and fall of powerful states and monarchs
- Daily life both in the cities and out in the fields
- The legacy of the Ancient Near East: religion, science, and writing systems.

Featuring a glossary, timeline, and suggestions for further reading, this book has all the tools the reader needs to understand the history and study of the Ancient Near East.

Daniel C. Snell is the L. J. Semrod Presidential Professor of History at the University of Oklahoma.

THE BASICS

ANCIENT NEAR EAST
THE BASICS

Daniel C. Snell

Routledge
Taylor & Francis Group

LONDON AND NEW YORK

First published 2014
by Routledge
2 Park Square, Milton Park, Abingdon, Oxon OX14 4RN

Simultaneously published in the USA and Canada
by Routledge
711 Third Avenue, New York, NY 10017

Routledge is an imprint of the Taylor & Francis Group, an informa business

British Library Cataloguing in Publication Data
A catalogue record for this book is available from the British Library

Library of Congress Cataloging in Publication Data
Snell, Daniel C.
Ancient Near East : the basics / Daniel C. Snell.
pages cm. -- (The basics)
"Simultaneously published in the USA and Canada"--Title page verso.
Includes bibliographical references.
1. Middle East--History--To 622. 2. Middle East--Civilization--To 622. I. Title.
DS62.2.S57 2013
939.4--dc23
2013004790

ISBN: 978-0-415-65697-9 (hbk)
ISBN: 978-0-415-65698-6 (pbk)
ISBN: 978-0-203-79832-4 (ebk)

Typeset in Bembo
by Taylor & Francis Books

Printed and bound by CPI Group (UK) Ltd, Croydon, CR0 4YY

For Marjorie Anctil and her Dennis,
Proving daily that there is never any reason to be bored
Because there is so much more to learn

CONTENTS

LIST OF FIGURES

All figures reproduced with kind permission of Adrienne Day.

ACKNOWLEDGMENTS

In the preparation of this work I again must express my appreciation to my wife, Dr. Katie Barwick-Snell, who reviewed every aspect of it as it was being revised, to our colleague and friend Adrienne Day, MfA, who created the original artwork, and to the staff at Routledge who saw it into final form. My long-suffering brother, David Snell, read a draft of the work and had valuable suggestions. As ever I am indebted to the stimulating environment of the University of Oklahoma's Department of History under the leadership of Dr. Robert Griswold for encouragement, and to the libraries of the University for the acquisition and borrowing of obscure tomes for my edification and amusement. None of the people or institutions mentioned is responsible for my errors.

I want to dedicate this work to my sister and her husband; Marjorie Snell Zack Anctil taught professionally for much of her life, and she exemplifies the dedication to the life of the mind.

DCS

Norman, Oklahoma, October 2012

WHAT WE MEAN WHEN WE TALK ABOUT THE ANCIENT NEAR EAST

Anyone who has studied even a little bit about the Middle East today has had the following conversation: Someone: Wow, the wars in the Middle East are constant. They are always fighting each other, and it seems as though it's been going on forever. You: Well, not exactly forever, and not with the same sides. Someone: But I mean, it goes back to the Bible, doesn't it, and long before? You: Not exactly.

And yet you remember the first Middle East war you paid attention to, back in 1967, when you were a freshman in college. The television was full of the build-up to the war, and both sides were talking tough. The television made it seem as though the clash was inevitable, and the outcome appeared to be headed toward all-out nuclear war, in which the United States would be pulled in as Israel's existence was threatened, and the Soviets would join as the Arabs' well-being was under attack.

But it was the end of the quarter. And you were invited over to the house of your young instructor, Alan Kimball, who would go on to make a career as a Russian specialist at the University of Oregon. Much later you would remind him of this day, which he had forgotten.

The whole class was worried about nuclear war, and the television did, in fact, show the tanks grinding across the desert. But Kimball

said, "In my lifetime I have seen this happen two times already."
He referred to the wars around the independence of Israel in 1948
and the Suez Crisis of 1956. "And it hasn't resulted in nuclear war.
You just need to take the long view. The great powers are
involved, but they are not suicidal, and the Middle Eastern powers
aren't either. It will eventually work itself out."

Kimball was right about that particular war, even though in the
very many years since the problems that created that war and the
problems that war created have not all been resolved. Is that
because the divisions run so deeply into history? Certainly there
are new factors that do not go back so very far, like nationalism and
the very existence of great powers that could intervene militarily.
These particular struggles are not eternal ones, but there were others,
many others, that defined how people in the region thought and
think about themselves and each other. Here we will try to sort some
of those out, though, no matter how superficially we try, we will
not get up to 1967 of our era.

The chapter title here is a riff on Raymond Carver's 1981 collection of short stories, *What We Talk About When We Talk About
Love*, which was a meditation on the things love can mean to
different people. Carver did not conclude that love meant any one
thing, and he did not imply that love was really self-serving, though
it always involved some sort of gratification.

By the Ancient Near East we mean the same thing as the Middle
East but in ancient times, down to the invasion of Alexander the
Great. Middle East is a term coined by the American naval writer
Alfred Mahan in a 1902 article. He wanted to differentiate the
regions of what most people then called the Orient, the East. The
Middle East did not include the Far East, meaning China and Japan,
and it also did not include India. In fact Mahan was talking about
"Middle" in the sense of latitude, not longitude, and implied that
what today we call the "Northern Tier" of the Middle East was a
separate entity that ought to be considered separately, including the
modern countries of Turkey, Iran, and Afghanistan.

His term caught on, and now all the languages of the region refer
to it as the Middle East. The term Near East probably originated in
Russia, where people were concerned for the East, the Orient, but
especially those areas near to themselves, meaning Iran and
Afghanistan, Armenia, and Turkey. But the term Near East persists

among scholars of the ancient world and means the whole area. The Orient too continues to be used, but it can be very extensive. And you will meet people in the Middle East who will say things like "You may not be able to understand us; we are Orientals." In the Western universities we still have institutions called Oriental Institutes, and the American Oriental Society, and those do encompass the scholars of the entire area, but these terms are relics of an American and European attitude that lumped the cultures together as "not us." They may still be "not us," but there are definitely distinctions to be made.

Students have told me, when they saw the titles of my books, that I needed to change them all to the Middle East, so people would know what we were talking about. But we do not do that, and in fact we persist in a terminological unclarity. Near to what? Near to us, in Russia and the rest of Europe. This seems unfair and culturally insensitive. Some suggest we should speak of Western Asia, which is more or less correct, but do we mean to include Egypt and the rest of North Africa? Most discussions of the ancient region do include Egypt, although the study of Egypt has evolved in different ways from that of the rest of the region.

What really were the boundaries? In ancient times geographical edges were not so important as centers, and so it is frequently difficult even to define political entities the way we do, by geographical features or imaginary lines on the ground. For ancient times we should not think in terms of borders but centers, and so we speak of clusters of places that seemed to be culturally similar.

The centers we are concerned with start in ancient Iraq. Southern Iraq was called in the first millennium *Abr Nahrain,* "across the two rivers" in Aramaic, then the common language of the region, and when the Greeks arrived and asked where they were, this got translated into "Mesopotamia," "Between Rivers." What this meant was not necessarily the area between the Tigris and Euphrates, but the area beyond the big bend in the Euphrates as it descends from Turkey through Syria and into Iraq. This whole region was a cultural unit in very ancient times. Consequently the term Mesopotamia, like Middle East, is slippery and expansive. The northern limit, though, is the Taurus Mountains in southern Turkey, and the eastern is the Zagros Mountains, which are shared between Iraq and Iran.

More to the west was a related cluster of centers which we call Syria-Palestine, naming it after later political entities. To the people in Mesopotamia it was simply the West. There were no geographical borders between the lower river valley that is now southern Iraq and the West, and the Euphrates flowed through to unite the two areas. And yet there were always geographic differences. The key difference was that in the West you could mostly do rainfall agriculture. The winter rains off the Mediterranean would give enough moisture to grow things, and the region is still famous for its wonderful olives and grapes. In Iraq you almost always needed to irrigate from the rivers, and you could not count on the rain, though some would come in the winter months, making the roads impassable.

Another region we include in the Ancient Near East is north of the Taurus Mountains, modern Turkey. This was part of early agricultural experiments and shared much with the more southern areas. But it too could survive on its rainfall and also on snow melt since its mountains did get snow in the winters. Another aspect of Turkey of interest to the ancients was its mineral wealth.

The Iranian highlands to the east were connected through trade to the other areas but were seen as distant and strange places. The mineral wealth there was of great value, though, to people farther west. Especially prized was lapis lazuli, a rich-looking blue stone that came from faraway Afghanistan. But it could be carried in small bits and fetched very high prices. It was used for jewelry and also for inlays on furniture as far away as Egypt.

The final area of focus is Egypt, which means not the whole extent of the modern country but rather the Nile River valley and its delta, sometimes a mere ten miles wide. New explorations in the eastern and western deserts have shown that in ancient times these areas were sparsely occupied, and yet the oases did furnish some agricultural goods. The climate in earlier times may have been wetter than now.

Modern students of the Middle East often include the rest of Africa north of the Sahara Desert on the cultural grounds that Islam spread across the continent, and there was certainly some significant contact with Egypt from Libya. But in ancient times our views are limited by the spread of writing, and we do not find writing to the west of Egypt, though we do find it south of Egypt in the Meroitic civilization in modern Sudan.

One area that was not significantly included in the Ancient Near East is the Arabian desert. For most of the period we are concerned with that desert was practically impassable. Only when camels were domesticated in the mid-first millennium did people go there much. The coast of the Arabian or Persian Gulf, however, had probably been visited by traders whenever southern Iraq could afford to buy spices and stones from distant places, and archaeological investigations there have produced important evidence of settlement originating in southern Iraq.

These are the regions we are interested in when we talk about the Ancient Near East, but as with love, we may mean different things when we talk to different people. And the more basic question of why we talk about the Ancient Near East, as with love, may involve our own self-interest. Edward Said in his 1978 book *Orientalism* charged that the study of the region was motivated by a desire to colonize it among the Western Powers; he examined particularly Britain and France, both of which did eventually establish supposedly temporary colonies sponsored by the League of Nations in the area after World War I.

Colleagues of mine were amazed to discover that the venerable American Oriental Society, of which I am myself a life member, had not changed its name because of Said's attack. But in several responses to his book and to derivative studies people who study the Middle and Near East have argued that choices of field and area of interest in the past as in the present were not dictated by imperial designs. Funding, of course, might be, but people come to study the region from Europe and the Americas for their own, mostly non-political reasons. Those reasons may be self-serving, and the prejudice against contemporary "Orientals" does sometimes crop up, especially in the works of Western visitors in the nineteenth and twentieth centuries. And on radio talk-shows even now you hear people talking about how "The Arab World" and similar entities are "a thousand years behind" us. Really? But they were so far ahead of "us" for such a very long time.

How this view might have developed we shall explore later on. But here we should clarify some of the geographical terms used over the three thousand or so years of this ancient history. The basic problem is that the peoples of the region called themselves and their geographical areas different things in different periods, and our terminology tries to follow theirs.

To begin with, Sumer meant the cities of southern Iraq, which were a cultural rather than a political unity. This term probably is reflected in the Bible in Shinar (Genesis 10:10, 11:2, 14:1). Sumer may have had some political meaning in that it stood for the members of a coalition of states that had a religious focus in the central Iraqi town of Nippur near Baghdad. The god who headed the religious pantheon was at home there, but it was never a political capital. The edges of Sumer are as usual not well defined. If we look to the Sumerian King List, which is a list of kings of city states written in the Sumerian language, Sumer may have stretched from the Iranian lowlands all the way upriver on the Euphrates to Mari, just inside the modern state of Syria. The Sumerian language was related to no other, and it may have been the one for which the cuneiform writing system was devised.

Akkad was north of Sumer, central Iraq now. It became important in the third millennium when people from there thrust into Sumer. Again, the borders of the region were left undefined. Here too there was a language named after the region, Akkadian, a Semitic language related to still living languages including Arabic and Hebrew.

Assyria was farther north still in Iraq and bled over into the modern states of Iran, Turkey, and Syria. This was an outpost of Mesopotamian culture that in the second millennium was a frontier area. It depended on rainfall agriculture, but some parts of Assyria were marginal in their rainfall, meaning in some years you could not have successful farming.

Syria was a term perhaps derived from the word Assyria, but it included the area to the west of northern Iraq all the way to the Mediterranean coast. In the fourth millennium already there was trade contact, and in many ways Syria was western Mesopotamia. It too relied on rainfall, with somewhat more success than Assyria. The term Syria became common in the first millennium referring to a number of small states in what is now Syria, Lebanon, and Israel and Palestine.

Anatolia is Greek for the area in which the sun rises from the Greek perspective, meaning modern Turkey. Dependent on rainfall agriculture, this mountainous region was isolated from the rest of the Near East in many periods, but the Taurus Mountains did have passes through them, and people from the south traded in Anatolia, and the Anatolians intervened in the south.

Palestine derives from the Egyptian and Hebrew term for the Philistines, people from the Aegean area who came to the coast of what is now the state of Israel and the Gaza Strip. They were the first peoples of the area the Romans encountered, and the Romans called the region behind the Philistines by their name too. This too is an area dependent on rainfall for agriculture.

Nubia was the Roman term for the area south of the first waterfall on the Nile as you go upriver. It was regarded by Egyptians as closely connected to Egypt, though in antiquity people there probably spoke different languages from Egyptian. Like Egypt Nubia got little rainfall and so was almost entirely dependent on the Nile's flood for irrigation and agricultural success. Modern Sudan encloses Nubia, but the modern state is much bigger.

The study of the Ancient Near East has in the past been focused on people who could write or at least whose leaders had access to writing. Writing represented a response to the need to manipulate surpluses, and so it is a cultural product that seems to underline the success of the peoples who used it. But writing was not accessible to most people living in the past, and it gives a narrow picture of human activity and achievement. Since the 1820s archaeological investigations have sought to supplement what we know from the writing of ancient peoples, and they have filled out some aspects of our understanding. Archaeology has allowed us to see much farther back than writing alone did, and we now see the Ancient Near East as the cradle of many of our own physical as well as intellectual successes. Though archaeology is getting more precise and is trying to ask and answer more sophisticated questions, the kinds of things we learn from archaeology do not necessarily directly supplement our study of written sources. Sculpture can depict how people wished to be seen, and how they conceived of their gods and other aspects of their environment. Before people could write, they could farm and build buildings, and they could express complicated systems of thought about death. But we do not come close to understanding what these were and what they meant before we have people writing about them.

Writing itself was a way to extend human memory, which may have gotten overloaded with a wealth of necessary detail as people were keeping track of more and more things. This sensory overload did not burden many people in any society, but you can see that the need to retrieve details about goods and workers might give rise to techniques to organize and to record them. Such inventions were not intended to last very long, but humans found them helpful, and we may be grateful that they actually did last a very long time, regardless of the intentions of the people who wrote.

Archaeology and writings give us the possibility of understanding what ancient people did and thought. These understandings can be very exciting and can sometimes explain the origins of some of our own ideas and practices, but we can understand only part of what they were doing and thinking. The lives and endeavors of most of our forebears are lost to us. And so we ought to be modest always in what we claim to know about the Ancient Near East.

We must look at one other dimension, time. Modern people date using the Christian Era, guessing that Christ was born about 2,000 years ago. This gives us a universal time scale, but it means that almost all the dates in this work are before it. We say BCE, meaning before the common era, since the era is used by people of many different religions. And for more recent times we say CE, common era, meaning the Christian era.

The ancients did not think in these ways. They dated by the years of the kings, and then they had to remember, sometimes through writing it down, what the order of the kings was. For us the use of the common era is convenient, but odd in that 2000 BCE happened before 1900 BCE, and we find ourselves moving down toward our own era instead of along through the historical periods as the ancients conceived of them. I tend to refer to absolute dates when possible and not to centuries, because using centuries introduces the same confusion we have in our era, where the nineteenth century after Christ has dates that start with 1800. We ought not to think, though, that our dating methods are really very precise. They are not; they are stabs and guesses and approximations, and they may change as we understand more about the chronology, meaning the succession of events and periods, in the region. I am sorry about this imprecision, but it does not mean that we are not on any firm basis for our dates. There is lots of converging evidence that we are approximately right, but the details will be refined by future study.

Timeline

	4000	3100	3050–2663	2663–2200	2160–2066	2066–1650	1650–1550	1550–1200	1200–800	800–600	600–539	539–330	330–30
Egypt	Pre-Dynastic	Early Dynastic	Early Dynastic	Old Kingdom	1st Intermediate	Middle Kingdom	2nd Intermediate	New Kingdom	3rd Intermediate	Neo-Assyrian	Neo-Babylonian	Persian	Alexander, Ptolemies
Iraq	Ubaid	Uruk	Early Dynastic	Early Dynastic, Old Akkadian	Gutian	Ur III, Old Babylonian	Old Babylonian	Babylonian, Middle Assyrian	Neo-Assyrian	Neo-Assyrian	Neo-Babylonian	Persian	Alexander, Seleucids
Syria		Uruk colonies		Ebla		Mari Palace			Neo-Hittites		Neo-Babylonian	Persian	Seleucids
Anatolia						Old Assyrian trade	Old Hittite	Hittite empire		Neo-Assyrian	Persian	Persian	Successors to Alexander
Israel									"Conquest"/United/Divided Kingdom	Neo-Assyrian	Babylonian Exile	Persian	Seleucids and Ptolemies

Map of the Ancient Near East

2

THE EARLY MILLENNIA

Let us begin with a fable. But unlike my other stories, this one has no textual basis and is in a sense only a flimsy guess explaining a basic fact of what people did in the Ancient Near East. It is like the Just-So Stories which the British author Rudyard Kipling wrote for children. They explained how the leopard got his spots in a reasonably coherent and pleasant way, but they would not work for biologists or anyone who knew much about leopards. My fable is based on a guess by archaeologists about why human beings domesticated plants and animals. This was the greatest and most lasting innovation in the Ancient Near East. Here is how it might have begun:

A Fable. Long ago and not so far away (say, 8000 BCE in northern Iraq), there lived a family which had been doing quite well, thank you. There was a man and his wife and there were their three sons and three daughters, and there were also a couple of uncles who lived with them. Their wives had died in childbirth. The couple had been very lucky because almost all the children had lived to adulthood; this rarely happened in that time or place.

But they did not live as you or I live, Best Beloved (so Kipling). No, they wandered. They had no houses, and when it rained, they stayed in the rain or huddled in caves or under the overhanging banks of rivers. And they picked berries and vegetables and roots and they hunted antelope. They lived in a place and time when there were two seasons, a wet rainy winter followed by a hot dry summer.

They knew where to go to find the best stands of wild growing plants, and they became a little protective of this knowledge. Each late spring when the wild wheat matured, they would visit their favorite stand and pick it clean. And each late summer when the antelopes began to move from the nearby desert, they made sure to be in position to kill many of them.

The eating was good, and the life was easy. It did not take more than six weeks to gather all the wheat they could use in the whole year. But of course they had to carry the wheat with them to the next place they wanted to visit.

By good fortune the boys found wives, and the girls found husbands, and, as these things go, they began to have children, and many of them lived beyond their first years.

The uncles were concerned, and even the father worried. Perhaps there will not be enough for everyone. The mother was upset. "Of course there will be enough; there has always been enough," she said.

The father said, "Yes, there has always been enough, but look at all the babies. Look at all the daughters-in-law and all the sons-in-law. This cannot go on. We must send them away."

"Send them away?" The mother said. "Why don't you leave first?" She said this to the least pleasant uncle. "Or you," she said to her husband, who looked away.

The mother thought it was a bad deal. She loved her grandchildren and liked to have them around. The father did too, she thought, but, a few weeks and a few moves later, the men, including the young ones, had all decided. The band would break up, and the young ones would no longer come along to the known areas in the upcountry. They would work their way down toward the plains and seek their luck down there.

The night before they were to go, the mother gathered her daughters and daughters-in-law around the fire. "My daughters, I know this may be hard," she said. "You will not find the good stands of wheat and the fat antelopes we are used to; you may have very slim pickings, especially until you know the country. You know we can't all survive here, and there may be beautiful, wonderful fields and valleys beyond."

The girls nodded sadly, some already with babies at their breasts, quite cute babies, though some sickly.

"But we know that wheat grows in its proper season from its seed, and I have saved some of the biggest and best from our last gathering, and here they are," she said with pride, showing the girls several small sacks of grain. "You go down and find likely places, and you plant the seeds and make sure they have water, and they may grow even as our ancestral stands have grown."

The girls looked doubtfully at the little sacks. They knew the mother had their welfare at heart and that she had always spoken against the separation.

Next morning the two groups parted, promising that they would find each other early the next summer at that very place, one of their favorites because the wheat stands were near and the running brook was full of fish.

The old woman fretted through the next year, and the elder band heard nothing from the youngsters. One of the uncles died, thank goodness, but there was more than enough to feed everybody.

When the appointed time came, the older group was camped at the lush brook, and there they came, the youngsters, looking on the whole quite well and well fed. There were some new babies, and the mother was very happy to see how big and healthy they were.

She and the daughters and the daughters-in-law convened to cook a meal, and the daughters and the daughters-in-law had brought along some wheat. But what wheat. Its kernels were much bigger than the mother had ever seen. Yes, the youngsters said, they had done as she had said. They had planted the seeds, they had made sure there was water, they had kept animals and humans away from them, and the wheat had grown much bigger and more luxuriant than they had ever before seen. The yield was three times greater than the wild wheat, and they had already planted the biggest kernels in hopes of an even larger crop.

The mother could not believe her eyes. The daughters and the daughters-in-law affirmed that the land below was not as good as the upland, but if you planted and took care of your food crops, you got much more than from the wild stands. The mother, when they prepared to leave after a few days of visiting and feasting, asked them for some of their seed grain and began herself to plant and water even in the uplands. The next holiday they celebrated together, everyone had bigger seeds. And the men had corralled some baby antelopes which they were raising to eat later.

And that, Best Beloved, may be how plants and animals were domesticated, not because people were actually starving, but because they thought they might later, because of what scholars call perceived scarcity. And the experimentations this called forth led to domestication, and domestication slowly, eventually, changed everything.

People had been coming through the region that became the Ancient Near East for millennia before we catch sight of them archaeologically. We know from genetics that biologically modern humans evolved in sub-Saharan Africa about 40,000 years ago, and they took the route of the Nile Valley into the rest of the world. But they were not sedentary and they did not practice agriculture. They were hunters and gatherers who followed animals and picked up fruits and vegetables.

We do not know how these people were organized, and they seem not to have used any very complex tools we can find. But we do know that in this very long period we call the Old Stone Age they created art on cave walls and probably had complex ideas about what we would call religion. The art may have been sympathetic magic, which showed hunters succeeding in killing animals, and thereby helped to make it so. When we find burials, we can see that these people assumed an afterlife for their loved ones since they buried them with things they might need in the future, with food and sometimes with tools.

The tools were chipped from flint, which was widely available, but the tools did not show much local variation. Though we assume that these people had use of one or more languages, we cannot know for sure what the languages were like. Modern human languages trace their origins back to much more recent periods.

We have lately come to see that our ancestors lived at the same time and in the same places as other hominoids we call Neanderthals, and they may have interbred with them occasionally. Why Neanderthals died out is unknown. But there were a number of global coolings accompanied by glaciations since 42,000 before the present, and these challenged all living beings who had gotten used to warmer climates. The advance of the polar glaciers carved new valleys where they came, and they may also have pushed rains farther south, so that some of the areas in the Near East that are now deserts were in earlier times lush and verdant. Presumably humans enjoyed those areas and moved away from the colder extremes.

AGRICULTURE—FROM THE HILLY FLANKS TO THE RIVER VALLEYS

The last cold period melted away between 10,000 and 8000 BCE in Europe and the Near East, and the rains probably moved north with the glaciers, leaving a climate much like the modern one in the region. There were rains that fell in the winter, wafted in from the Mediterranean Sea, but in the summers there would be no rain, and the temperatures could become extreme.

The retreat of glaciers, which never had gotten as far south as the Near East, and the drift of the rains, seem not to have affected how humans lived. They continued to gather what they could and to follow animals as they explored more northern areas. An experiment in the Turkish mountains in the 1950s showed that a small group could gather enough wild grain in six weeks of strenuous work to supply their needs for calories for an entire year. This might lead to a porridge-only diet of great boringness, and yet it was a good beginning to not starving. This raises the question why hunters and gatherers would stop being hunters and gatherers at all; work six weeks, and you're done, except for the fixings of meat and fruit and nuts, which could be harvested seasonally.

We call this period the Mesolithic because its inhabitants showed lots of quick innovation in their stone tools in contrast to the earlier ages, and this "Middle Stone" Age was trying new things out, perhaps with a view to more efficient use of the things they found and killed. Again there does not seem to be much regional variation in their tools, meaning perhaps that they did have different languages and cultures, but the ways they got and prepared food were pretty much the same.

But something changed, not at the same time everywhere but gradually in some places, and our guess is that what changed was the success at having babies that lived. Infant death was probably astronomically high, and women had to have many pregnancies to assure that one or two children made it to the age of reproduction themselves. The survival of the group depended on keeping women pregnant, though they may also have been responsible as the chief gatherers of food; men may have been more likely to be sent off to the hunt since children could do without them for a day or two, but children would not thrive without their mothers.

We are guessing about demography in these early societies, of course, and we do not know why now, of all times and places, child mortality should be declining, but gradually it did decline. This was happy news for our ancestors since it gave them more workers to do the hunting and gathering and to care for later children.

Another related development may have been increased longevity for a few of the parents. This gave children the all-important grand-mothers, who could care for them and free up their mothers for more distant gathering while also imparting to the children a greater depth of memory than previously had been possible. Grandfathers too may have been important in passing down lore about hunting places and practices.

We imagine that the proliferation of mouths to feed, both old and young, led some groups to feel population pressure, meaning they felt that they could not reliably feed all their numbers with the hunting and gathering they were doing. Climate variations too might have inspired such ideas. A dry year in northern Iraq nowa-days can be very distressing to farmers; it may have been terrifying for hunters and gatherers.

These people expanded their technologies and experimented more systematically with domestication, that is, adopting plants and animals for their own needs. Doubtless it had been known for a long time how grains grew, and people had carried seeds from one place to another, but now some of them started planting them in places they intended to return to. Something like the fable at the start of this chapter may have happened, probably in several places and times. And some animals too seemed more useful than others to have around.

Dogs had been adapted to humans for quite some time, maybe first in Central Asia. Now sheep were trapped and penned and bred, selected for their wool and for their milk. Pigs too were early domesticated, and this may have been quite a task, to judge from how ornery wild boars can be. And the cow, probably not so big and mean as some modern bulls, also found itself controlled by humans. Later, when you needed to make sure mice and other vermin did not attack the grain you had stored, the Egyptians tried to tame that untamable mouser, the cat.

You chose plants that were at home in the climate you had, but you could select them too for features you liked. Emmer wheat was chosen for bigger grains and for easier husking. The interesting thing about these efforts was that they were shared across the Near East. Sheep that were wild on the Iranian foothills showed up within a thousand years in the valley of the Jordan River, 600 miles or 960 kilometers on the other side of the Near East. And grain at home by the Jordan was harvested in Iraq within the same period.

Again, we cannot be sure that all these people understood the same languages or had the same ideas about what they were doing, but they certainly were sharing. They also shared stone tool technology, and that technology proliferated new shapes with new purposes. These were specialized tools for particular purposes, scrapers for leather from animals you had killed, maybe for their meat, but you certainly did not allow the leather to rot when it could be so usefully manipulated. These stoneware developments give the name Neolithic, "New Stone," to the period, and these tools never stopped changing and adapting to new tasks.

We call the areas where these innovations were taking place the Hilly Flanks, meaning not the highest mountains of the region, but the foothills, where rainfall was caught by the mountains to allow a winter growing season, and where the grazing animals could be sure of finding food. The process of domestication of plants and of animals we call the Neolithic Revolution, but these changes were not really very quick and probably were imperceptible to the people living through them. And hunting and gathering continued, with agriculture and animal husbandry at first as supplemental, and then in some places they became primary.

Scholars used to think that the Neolithic Revolution was linked closely with sedentism, the decision to live in one place, but now we are not so sure. There were some towns, like Jericho in the Jordan Valley, that relied on trading salt and seem at first not to have had any domestic animals or plants; hunters and gatherers exchanged their finds for Jericho's minerals, and that allowed a few hundred people to live in one lucrative place.

Logically there is no reason you would have to live in only one place. People had been wandering among known stands of grains, fruits, and likely hunting grounds for millennia, and they probably kept on doing that even if they had planted some of the crops and brought along some of the animals. But there was the problem of poaching, of other human groups encroaching on grounds where your group had worked. And so people stayed and built houses of mud brick which were intended to be permanent. They might still take a hunting vacation, especially the men, but they certainly did not want to cede their rights to do agriculture in places where the investment of time had been made.

We call these settled places early village communities, and their very existence began a process of making human society more complex than it ever had been before. A change that eventually set in was differentiation in people's jobs. Agriculture turned out to be so very productive that not everyone needed to be a farmer full time, and craftsmen began to specialize, first in stone, and then in other materials. Eventually there were almost full-time practitioners of religious rites. Also there may have been full-time government employees who were busy with collecting surplus agricultural produce and redistributing it. Human social hierarchy proliferated. Some hierarchy probably always had existed in the sense that people had different talents and personalities, and with the growth of hierarchy grew some of the ills to which we are still heirs, like the oppressiveness of the wealthy and the suffering of the poor.

Not all was positive in this transition to agriculture, even if we ignore social hierarchies. People's teeth got worse perhaps because of an overreliance on grains and the inadvertent inclusion of rock grit. Domesticated animals too may have deteriorated on a more monotonous diet, and the faces of pigs collapsed in the process. The world of the early settled villages does not appear to have been threatened by raids by other groups, since people did not build walls around their settlements, but a change in a river's course, or a bad drought, or any other mishap could cause people to think about abandoning this village. It might even inspire them to retreat into hunting and gathering.

They might also pursue a new option, which depended on their domesticated animals, and follow them where the forage was good, picking up some vegetables and fruits on the way and indulging in hunting when possible. This style of life was not the same as the earlier hunting and gathering, and we call it nomadism, implying a wandering path. When we study more recent nomads, though, we see that they do not wander aimlessly but in set patterns, which follow the seasons and the likely watering holes and grazing areas. When exactly a nomadic group visited one of its haunts could not be predicted, but the order of the moves could be.

Another byproduct of early settled village agriculture was productive for modern archaeologists. That is pottery, which may have started as a way of making baskets more permanent and capable of being used to cook over fires. The earliest pottery does look like baskets, but it developed quickly into other shapes and uses, beakers and storage jars, and cups and plates. The interesting thing is that the styles of what people liked changed gradually. Pottery allows us for the first time perhaps to see individual cultures of people, or at least of craftsmen. The identification of ethnic groups with pottery is very problematic; by that measure we are all Chinese now—look at the bottom of your teacup! A great thing about pottery is that it wears out and is thrown away, and in ancient conditions it was not carried very far from where it broke. And so sometimes we can identify the function of rooms from the pots discarded there. And we can date sites at least relatively if they were using the same pottery; this means that we can say they were roughly contemporary, though we may not be able to say exactly when that was according to our modern reckoning of years.

We can identify ruins mainly made by humans by the presence of broken pottery. And since World War II this fact has allowed us to embark on efforts to identify just from the surfaces when, more or less, ruins were occupied. We call this surface survey, and there are built-in inaccuracies in it since not everything ever used at the site is likely to be found on the modern surface, but it does give a general idea and has proved useful in trying to reconstruct the courses of rivers and canals even when they may have meandered away from their ancient beds.

The Neolithic Revolution spread gradually from its initial sites in the hills of the Zagros, the Amanus, and Lebanon, and by 4000 BCE may have gotten as far as Greece. But other hunters and gatherers were elsewhere moving toward the domestication of plants and animals in their own areas, and there were other domestication revolutions in East Asia and South America later. Still, the animals and plants tamed by Ancient Near Eastern peoples remain the basic ones still exploited in Europe and the Americas.

CITIES—LIFE ON THE PLAINS

Agriculture's productivity continued to allow more babies to live and more people to attain a venerable old age, and so the populations of the village communities gradually grew. Again we imagine a perceived population pressure, not that in any place the human population came close to the numbers of people who live in the modern Middle East. The earlier response to population had been to delve into domestication, and the response now was to spread out, even down into the forbiddingly hot river valleys of the Euphrates and the Tigris in Syria and Iraq.

It did rain in those valleys, but not reliably, and so you had to resort to irrigation. The efficiency of watering plants must have been figured out long before, but it became essential to do that in Iraq. Again humans were confronted with a surprise: irrigated plants got much bigger yields than rainfall-fed plants, and plants gave as much as ten times the volume of food. Irrigation was fairly simple on the banks of the Euphrates, where all you needed to do was to break the levy and water would flow into riverside fields.

The disadvantage to irrigation only became obvious after several generations as the water left salts on the surface and the fields might become unusable. This development caused a move toward barley as a crop since barley is more resistant to salts. Salinization can be overcome by totally flushing the land periodically. That took a lot of water, and sometimes it seemed wiser just to move on to other fields. The variable in southern Iraq was where water was available; there was always more than enough land.

For a couple of thousand years the settled village farmers replicated their upland life of seasonal agriculture down in the river valleys, but complexity was increasing. One place we see this is in the southern city of Eridu. There we find large public buildings that functioned as temples; they were larger than normal houses and had signs of things being stored within. Temples later were not just places for worship, if they were ever chiefly that, but places where the community redistributed goods to people who needed them; that is, like our churches, mosques, and synagogues, they were centers for charity and for resource sharing.

CITY STATES—PATRIOTISM OF THE SMALL STATE

When settled farming communities developed in the river valleys, none of them seems to have been much larger than any other, but after a couple of thousand years there did develop different growth patterns. We name the period that showed the most extensive growth the Uruk period after its largest site, known in the Bible as Erech (Genesis 10:10). It was a couple of miles across and may have had a population as large as 40,000 people, and its effect on surrounding communities was significant. Smaller towns were sucked into the big city. The farmers continued to farm the same fields, but they lived in town and went out daily to their work. The tax revenues and other contributions from such a large number of people allowed much more grandiose projects. In Uruk this surplus was spent on the precinct where temples were concentrated; a high platform was built to be the foundation of the temple buildings, and the buildings themselves were made snazzy with dazzling colored mud brick outside and in.

Uruk was a wonder of the world, but other cities were also growing, and this raises the question of why. The environment did not apparently change, though farmers were getting more and more productive as they mastered irrigation. And such concentrations of people raised many problems that had not had to be faced before. Sanitation, mere waste disposal, must have been a major problem, and the fact that pigs will eat anything, and dogs almost anything, helped, but they may not have made these early cities very pleasant.

Pleasant was not the point. Cities were always places where new diseases could take hold and spread more easily than in the country. Interaction was probably the attraction. People came to the city with new products and ideas. The city was a bigger market for everything, and fortunes could be more easily made than in the plodding life of agriculture. Also power could be had there if you could get your fellows to join you in enterprises, of building, or of war.

How did institutions get surpluses in goods? It may have been a matter of taxation, meaning the group authority decided on the amounts and went around and made sure taxes were paid. Or it may have been as a result of freewill offerings, when people thanked the gods for their successes. Coercion and ideology could both have been involved, but this resource pooling was essential for any large-scale project, and many were in the offing.

The people who directed these enterprises concentrated surplus things, but they also insisted that people give some of their labor to the enterprises. This way of using forced labor, or at least volunteer labor that was not exactly given freely, was typical of the development of other polities, and it remained a feature of governments in the Middle East almost to modern times.

One innovation that came out of the Uruk period was writing. This technique for memory extension started in texts that recorded economic data and were not meant to be kept around very long. These texts began as little pillows of clay with numbers on them, and you were supposed to be able to remember what the numbers stood for. But later people wrote signs probably standing for entire words to say exactly what the numbers were counting. These were pictographic, and sometimes we can guess what they were meant to represent. A similar process was happening in early Egypt leading to hieroglyphics, where the earliest writing was on stone tags with holes through them; probably they were attached to bags full of whatever was being delivered.

Writing arose in the context of record-keeping and did not get used much beyond that purpose for a long time. Scribes wanted to record items they were counting, but they also wanted to write down people's names, and for that they developed innovative devices to use the sounds of objects to write similar sounds in names. In Sumerian they noticed that the word for *water* /a/ was similar in sound to the word for *in*, also /a/ but put at the end of a noun. The trend toward using signs not just for their word value but also for their sound value seems to be a creative trend in the history of writing. It allowed flexibility and innovation.

These developments in Mesopotamia were happening as early as 3100 BCE, and during the next five hundred years the flexibility of the system increased and it changed the way it looked. It started as drawings on clay tablets, but it became increasingly wedge-shaped, perhaps because the stylus used to inscribe the signs changed, or perhaps because it was discovered to be quicker to write shapes only of one style. This nail-shaped writing became standard in southern Iraq, but it made the signs more abstract and less recognizable as pictures.

We should not exaggerate the difficulty of the cuneiform, nail-shaped, system since in most periods only about 120 signs were in common use. This means that it rivals the basic Japanese syllabary in difficulty, and Japanese first-graders have no problem with that. A syllabary is a set of signs that stand for syllables, and that is what the Mesopotamians developed.

There were people who spoke Sumerian, but there were others whose names made sense in another language, Akkadian, which is related to other Semitic languages. That was the key to the decipherment of Akkadian in modern times, and in ancient times there were scribes whose names were Akkadian as well as many whose names were Sumerian. But there were other people whose names were in other languages. You could sound them out, though, and that is what scribes did.

Sumerian may be related to no other language, though there are some scholars who want to connect it to the Dravidian languages of modern south India. It would make sense that there might be some link across the Indian Ocean since we know there was trade there in historical times, but the evidence is not good for a relationship to Sumerian, and so we treat it as if it were linguistically isolated.

We are helped in our understanding of Sumerian by the fact that it died out early as a spoken language, though when exactly no one knows. It retained its cultural value for people in southern Mesopotamia so that Akkadian speakers wanted to learn it and to write in it. This is the origin of the dictionary making in which they engaged. These texts give us insight into how later scribes understood Sumerian.

At first the dictionaries consisted only of lists of signs that a beginning writer should know. Later scribes added translations of the most frequent phrases into Akkadian, though sometimes they simplified what the Sumerians had written. They grouped together similar signs sometimes, and other times they brought together the names of all known trees and woods. It is hard to look things up in these works, and only modern scholarship has tried to index them using our phonetic writing system. The point was to retain this knowledge for later reference.

In Egypt writing was first used for record-keeping. But there quickly it was extended to label pictures in monuments, meaning plaques, usually on stone, that were meant to last for a very long time to commemorate important people and events. There were connections to Mesopotamia, perhaps by sea along the Red Sea, and though the writing systems were different, the idea of having such a system may have been borrowed in one direction or the other.

In Egypt too, signs began as pictures of objects. But people's names were needed too. There may have been somewhat less linguistic variety in people's names than in Mesopotamia, and again we have difficulty understanding the names written. As in Iraq names may have inspired scribes to use signs as more phonetic indicators. Here what was being represented was less clearly a set of syllables, but there was the added problem that vowels did not seem so important in the ancient Egyptian language, and so there was no easy way of showing them.

Egyptian was distantly related to the Semitic languages, and to nearby African languages, and the idea that the significant features of words were conveyed in their consonants was one shared in some of those languages. Since no vowels were represented, though there were vowels pronounced, the Egyptian system was inherently ambivalent, and our understanding especially of its verbal system is hampered by its writing.

The history of cities in Egypt is much less clear than in Iraq, partly because Egyptians are still living exactly where ancient Egyptians lived. Monumental buildings have been preserved because most of them were built in the desert on the fringes of the cultivated areas to avoid the yearly summer floods. But more lowly structures have been destroyed over time, and so our impression of urban centers is limited.

TERRITORIAL EMPIRES—THE FOUR QUARTERS UNITED

What happened next is easier to understand in Egypt than in Iraq. In Egypt a leader from the middle part of the country got the idea of conquering all the other parts, and he was able to beat them all into submission because the Nile was the lifeblood of Egypt. If you could control the commerce on the Nile, you could tax it and you could stop it. The only difficult part was the Delta, where the river split into several streams; this area was highly productive and not easily united. But with surplus goods and armed men from Upper Egypt the Delta, or Lower Egypt, succumbed.

The upriver leaders set up a new city as the administrative capital, not upstream in their home district, but at the apex of the Delta. This location allowed easier collection of taxes from the Delta and also redistribution, and the king could dart off in any threatened direction if he needed to. The place was first called "The White Wall," and later "Firm is the beauty of the Sun-God," in Egyptian *Mn-nfr-R^c*, which the much later Greeks heard as Memphis.

The process of unifying Egypt turned out to be fairly easy, the product of a few generations of committed rulers, and the standards that they set for rulership and for art continued to be the foundation of what later Egyptians valued. Who the first successful king was remains unclear, but there is a palette, a stone plate used for mixing make-up, probably kohl, an eye shadow. The palette shows the ruler called "Hammer-Fish," in Egyptian, Narmer, decapitating people from the north of Egypt (see Figure 6.1, p. 97). This is a pretty object of art, but it clearly was not a pretty process.

The idea that there should be only one ruler for the whole river valley was established by this unification and continued to be the Egyptian political ideal even when the reality was different. The king saw himself as embodying this unity, pulling together the Delta and the upriver country, with his own two hands. He was depicted as strong and solid and devoted to his role. Few human peculiarities were allowed to intrude, and when he was shown with a wife, even her presence did not humanize him but merely indicated her dependence on him. It is hard for us to get behind the clichés of the depictions of kings, both in sculpture and in words; the kings were presented as stereotypes, and each one had to be as stereotypically strong and magnificent as his predecessor.

The process of identification of gods from different places with each other and the elaboration of an Egypt-wide pantheon may have predated the political unification. With the rise of a single ruler, though, the process accelerated, and the king was supposed to be the chief priest of all the important gods. He could not be in all places for all ceremonies, and so he appointed priests and administrators across the country. A theme of ancient Egyptian history was the tension between the royal center and the scattered shrines and the effort of the priests at the shrines to have their sons follow them in office. Central administrators preferred regulating who in the next generation got the king's favor. The kings and their lackeys feared that well-entrenched local worthies could rival them for control of regions. And that did happen in later history. The usual assumption in Egypt was that a son would follow a father into a given job, just as the king usually followed his father. Women too followed the work of their mothers, and on rare occasions they did have access to powerful offices; we know of several queens who ruled as regents when their young sons or other male relatives were too young or otherwise not qualified to rule.

The situation in Iraq was more complex. There the larger cities established reputations as regional powers which could affect what smaller places did. The larger centers competed with each other for more towns that could serve as tribute-suppliers, and they also warred with each other. This led in the Early Dynastic Period, about 3000 down to 2400 BCE, to cities building walls around themselves, where outlying towns could find refuge when invaders came.

The wars we know best were those between the cities of Lagash, over to the east of the rivers, and Umma, a close neighbor. They fought over an agricultural area which they both claimed. This fight lasted generations and finally ended with Umma overcoming Lagash. The Umma ruler, Lugalzagesi, saw this success as an opening to assert his authority throughout the southern plain, and he began to forge a larger state that ruled other previously independent entities.

Lugalzagesi's successes were the first hint of later imperialism. Though he may have been the first to act on the idea that one state should dominate, he was not long allowed to enjoy the fruits of his conquest.

A king with an Akkadian name, Sargon, had collected northern cities together and used the fighting men he got from them to sweep into the south. Southerners resisted, but Sargon had more fighters and was able to beat the southern cities. He did not always send the leaders into exile as prisoners, as he said he did to Lugalzagesi. Sometimes he reinstated the city ruler in his same city, probably to try to attract the local elite to Sargon's cause. This may have worked initially, but there were several rebellions against him and against his dynasty. People did not necessarily like being folded into his empire.

Later stories said that Sargon campaigned as far away as central Anatolia, now Turkey. He did get up to the Habur River in Syria and probably had something to do with the destruction of the city of Ebla, far to the west in central Syria. Campaigning might just mean raiding and withdrawing afterwards with booty, but in some places it meant establishing garrisons and administrators to get an ongoing cut of local agricultural produce. Administrative tablets on clay, sometimes in the Akkadian language in the cuneiform system, showed a central administration concerned about the eastern frontier as well as a wide range of trade goods.

Royal inscriptions left by Sargon and his descendants reveal a set of new ideas. These kings claimed to be "king of the four quarters," meaning the four directions relevant in the river valley—upriver, toward the Persian or Arabian Gulf, toward the mountains, and toward the desert. This title means that the kings claimed rulership of the whole civilized world as they knew it. To us such a claim seems outrageous, especially since they were not aware of Egypt. This claim caught the imagination of later rulers, and to rule the entire world became an ideal for them too.

Why would you want to do that? Attracting trade to the cities under your control seems to have been important to these kings, and they recognized that there were military costs to be paid for this power. There were social and physical costs too; one inscription says Sargon had 5,400 men who ate at his table. The picture conjured up shows the burden of such kingship; lots of people would want to work for you, and you would have to feed them.

The key to empires has always been recruiting collaborators. Communication was slow across the Ancient Near East, and getting the word back that some far place had rebelled would take a month or two at best. Putting the army together to punish the rebels might take another few months, and then they would have to boat out or just to walk out to wherever the empire had to be defended. For this to work you needed local elites to be committed to your rule, and for that they had to benefit in concrete ways from your power.

The size of Sargon's table along with his political tasks raises another feature of Ancient Near Eastern kingship. That is that kings could not stay in one place. We may say that some city was the capital, but that does not mean that the king was mostly there. Instead he needed to be on the road first to assure that his followers would not unduly burden his collaborators around Mesopotamia by eating them out of house and home and every kind of surplus. The king also needed to check up on what was happening in each locality, and to do so in sufficient force so as to be able to suppress things he did not like. We have buildings that were palaces, that is, residences of rulers not connected to the religious establishments, in several cities just before Sargon, and yet the king was mostly out and about, managing by walking around. A burden of this lifestyle was that he had to carry a lot of precious goods, the essence of his treasury, along with him, both for safekeeping and for rewarding his trusty servants. This was a world where there were no locks and keys, where treasury doors could only be sealed with clay and stamped to make sure they had not been opened. But robbers had no scruples about such barriers, and so the king traveled heavy with lots of guards.

Did he have a standing army? This is such an important feature of modern states that it is hard for us to imagine successful empires of the past without it. Probably he did have a faithful guard with whom he traveled, but most soldiers were seasonal workers. They went home in the winter, when the roads were difficult anyway because of the rains that turned them into mud, and they farmed crops for their families. In later periods such soldiers held their land from the king, and it was the greater part of their salary, though they probably were fed by the king when on duty.

Another part of royal ideology that lingered was the idea that the king was a god. Earlier city rulers had claimed to have been appointed by the gods of their cities and so to have been specially selected to do the gods' will, but they did not claim divine status for themselves. Sargon and his two sons did not claim that privilege either, but a grandson, Naram-Sin, did. That claim was not controversial in his lifetime, and he had a remarkably successful reign, reconquering distant Ebla and making a treaty with a ruler in Elam in Iran. He claimed to be larger than life, and he may have wanted to remove some of the city rulers that his kin had left in place in the southern cities; to remove people who had been appointed by gods may have shocked southerners. And though they probably did not buy the idea that the Akkadian ruler had gotten a sudden divine promotion, it might have placated some of his collaborators who could argue to their dependents that the king was like a god in his power.

In spite of his actual success in suppressing a rebellion and extending his grandfather's conquests, Naram-Sin went down in Mesopotamian tradition as a bad guy. He was not the last ruler of the dynasty, but he was the last memorable one, and later traditionalists blamed him and his impiety for the fall of the dynasty. Claiming to be a god himself was not chalked up as one of his sins; scribes instead claimed he was not properly taking care of the great god Enlil, an unlikely thing to accuse any Mesopotamian ruler of since it would be a public violation of the king's duty to show piety. His overweening pride may have been part of the bad reputation, not that this kept later rulers from also assuming the divine mantle. What this meant ranged from having temples built to you, to just writing your name with the divine determinative before it; the determinative might not have been actually pronounced when addressing the king.

One other aspect of Akkadian rule has left interesting traces. Even though the king had conquered most of the good agricultural land, he did not own it. We know this because one of Sargon's sons had a large stone monument made with purchases of land recorded. The king was buying, and groups of people were selling, presumably meaning that the land had been held communally by extended families, and the king was trying to increase his own holdings. This monument shows that the power even of these kings was not absolute; they could not confiscate everything. They had to pay real silver and real garments for it.

KINGS AND TEMPLES—CO-OPTATION OF THE GODS

The connection between gods and kings was close, but the economic significance of this may have been more important than the ideological meaning. Kings sometimes depicted themselves as intercessors between the divine realm represented by the very highest gods and the human realm, though there would have been lots of demons and spirits and personal and family gods in play too. Practically the kings usually strived to administer the temples themselves.

Temples were seen as very old and very prestigious households, and the kings were latecomers. An outdated modern model of Mesopotamian development argued that the people who emerged as kings had started as priests, but the evidence is not really clear. Kings seemed to be war leaders, and the early priests were not organizing defense or offense, but they were redistributing surpluses.

The surpluses came into temples from freewill offerings which people made in thanks for successes of various kinds; we can see the traces of these in what we call votive objects, things given to the temple like statues of a person, perhaps in fulfillment of a vow, promising the offering if something good happened, recovery from a disease, or successful birth of a baby who lived past early childhood.

Another source of goods and probably services too for the temple came from forced donations that we can see as taxes and that peasant farmers may have seen as insurance payments. These were probably mostly foods that could be stored and were redistributed to people in need. The people in need in turn might owe labor to the temple, but at least they were fed; in later eras the temple bought the people themselves and put them to work processing textiles, using the wool from temple sheep.

Temples were centers for charity as well as for religious devotion, though the religious devotion is hard to see except in the votive gifts that lasted. Many temples gave no access at all to ordinary people into their holy places. Statues of the gods, or their symbols, may have been brought out at great festivals, but usually they lived in pure and holy seclusion. Statues were sometimes taken on trips, though, like the human kings, to keep track of their friends and relations, and on those occasions normal people might have been able to catch auspicious glimpses of the gods.

In both Mesopotamia and in Egypt temples were not subject to taxation, meaning exactions from the government. The rationale probably was very like our exemption of churches, synagogues, mosques, and—let's get personal—universities and schools. We hold that such institutions are doing good charitable work and helping people who otherwise would be either destitute or, worse, uneducated, and so we do not ask them for money. In the ancient world such institutions can be seen as pious endowments, into which rich families could put their wealth in order to help the community at large but also to keep from paying what they might otherwise be expected to pay to the government.

In Egypt these endowments became a real problem in that large amounts of the wealth of the land were held by temples and could not be taxed by the government. It may be that the New Kingdom religious reforms were attempts at getting at that pent-up wealth. These surplus dedicated things included not just food but also land and the peasants working the land; they would be dedicated in perpetuity to the temples and so would not be subject to normal demands for forced labor and other taxes. The endowments were an element for stability, but they also limited what kings could do without interfering with them.

Kings could control and to an extent co-opt the endowments by controlling who got to administer them. We noted that the Egyptian king was supposed to be the chief celebrant and priest in every temple, but in fact he appointed people he liked to run them. There was a tendency toward occupational inheritance, as seen above, and so frequently he was stuck with either incompetents or with people who did not share his ideas about how the stored resources should be used.

This problem was less acute in Mesopotamia, perhaps because of the advent of newcomers in most periods who might not support the old-time religion in its every aspect. Kings may have felt more ready to intervene in temples than in Egypt, and there did not seem to be any such church and state conflict as we have in modern history except, perhaps, in the reign of the very last native-born Mesopotamian king, where the alienated temple establishment cooperated with his overthrow.

PYRAMIDS AND ZIGGURATS—MONUMENTS FOR THE AGES

The ultimate in pious endowments was enormous building projects. Irrigation works were sometimes focuses of community and state construction; making more land able to be watered was good for everyone. From the sluggishly moving Euphrates it was easy to breach the levy and flood nearby fields, and it did not take much organization to keep such systems going. Kings liked to be known for digging and cleaning canals. In Egypt the Nile itself provided the irrigation, but there is one early depiction of a king working on canals because agricultural production could be increased by getting water to the edges of the desert.

Building temples and walls was the goal of early kings, and in Egypt, because people were buried in the western desert and not in the flood plain, we have found elaborate tombs. Mesopotamians spent resources from time to time on royal tombs too, but burial did not develop into a powerful industry as it did in Egypt. The ideas about death were different in the two river valleys, and that may have been a reason that kings spent money more ostentatiously on tombs in Egypt than in Mesopotamia.

Elite Egyptians thought that people when they died followed the sun in its daily course and moved as it did into the west. They guessed that in the world of the dead life would continue more or less as it had in Egypt. You would need your body; you would need food; you would like to have some of the objects that had delighted you in the course of your life in Egypt. True, your physical body remained in your tomb, as did the accoutrements, but it was important that tombs be as well decked out as a person could afford.

These ideas led to the building of elaborate mounded buildings that are now called *mastaba*s from an Arabic word for "bench" because they look like benches. The body was buried below them, and there was also a chapel where surviving relatives could come and leave offerings for the deceased. When food was left, it decayed, and inscriptions indicate that it was all right not to leave food; the deceased would benefit if you only said the words for items of food. So spiritual food would do, and it was the thought that counted.

There were tombs of kings built as benches, but there were also tombs of many other worthies who could afford such things, and there were cemeteries that center on the kings. The idea may have been that the king was definitely going to make it into the blessed west, and so it would be smart to have yourself buried near him; we will all go together. A couple of early royal tombs go further still and contain the corpses of servants killed in order to accompany their lord in death. This practice presumably reduced the readiness of some Egyptians who had a choice to serve the king, and it was not pursued long.

What happened when there were few survivors in a family, or none at all? Fancy tombs had farms and peasants attached to them to support them and the live people who served in the tombs and the temples. Tombs were pious endowments that were intended to last forever. The hope was that priests would stand for all time before the deceased and make sure that food and drink were at least mentioned and possibly physically supplied.

Mummification was practiced from early times, but not consistently, and techniques for physically preserving the body improved in the course of Egyptian history. The Greek historian Herodotus who probably visited Egypt before 430 BCE said in his day there were three levels of mummification, varying by completeness and by cost. Cheapest was the method where the corpse was dried by being buried in salt for a couple of months. More expensively the corpse was buried in salt after having had the stomach and other internal organs extracted. Most expensive was the technique where the organs were extracted and replaced with fine spices.

In Mesopotamia in all periods the idea of death was like the Greek idea of Hades; everyone went to the same dismal place, regardless of status or achievements during life. Preservation of the body was not a goal, and though there definitely was thought to be some existence of the person after death, it was shadowy and unpleasant. Though your favorite things could be buried with you, it would not matter much where you were going, and so time and money were not expended on such preparations.

Work on tombs may not have been a major focus of Egyptians either, but it is the one we can still see because tombs were built beyond the flood plain in the western desert. In a few generations during the Fourth Dynasty of the Old Kingdom royal tombs went through an experimental elaboration that led to the building of the most elaborate tombs ever.

It started with a king called Djoser, meaning "The Pious." He had a *mastaba* built about 300 feet or 100 meters long. If you did not finish your tomb before you died, you would be buried in it unfinished. And work stopped as soon as you died. But Djoser had plenty of time. At first he expanded the *mastaba* upwards with several more similar structures, and then he added a couple more to create what we call a step pyramid, an enormous structure to cover his tomb, but not exactly pyramidal in shape. It ended up being 358 by

410 feet or 109 by 125 meters, and 203 feet tall or 62 meters. Nearby and under the pyramid he allowed many other people to prepare their tombs, probably his honored courtiers who did not have to give up their lives just when the king died. Djoser also built an elaborate village next to his pyramid, but it was not a normal village; it was only a façade of the buildings of a town, and its function was to give the king a place to perform his jubilee festival, a public ceremony in which he regained or asserted his vigor. In later times kings celebrated jubilees after they reigned thirty years, but that custom may not have been in effect for Djoser.

Subsequent kings did not even start out with a *mastaba*, but began with a pyramid in mind. They moved tons of blocks quarried near the tomb site, and it must have taken years to get these structures together. The Egyptians were winging it, though, trying out new techniques and seeing if they worked. You can see this with the three pyramids of Sneferu, a king whose name aptly means "Improvement." He started out with a very steep structure which may have collapsed during construction; this he abandoned and worked on another, and he modified the top to be at a gentler angle. Then he built another, with a gentle 45 degree angle which ended up being stable and lasting.

But in a generation Sneferu's efforts would be dwarfed by three generations of kings who built the great pyramids. The first of these, that of Khufu (whose name is short for "He [a god] has appeared"), is the largest, and it shows still some hesitation about where the king was to be buried. There is an underground tomb, which may have been the first plan, and then within the pyramid itself above ground level is another, later tomb chamber.

The second great pyramid, that of Khefren (meaning "His [a god's] name appears"), still has at its top a mantle of shiny stone over the large blocks that make up the pyramid. It is likely that when they were new each of the great pyramids had such a mantle, and they must have reflected the sun magnificently in their shiny surfaces. Weather has eroded the mantles, as well as the activities of later humans who liked to reuse the mantles in their punier buildings.

The Khefren pyramid has a temple right near the pyramid, where offerings to the king were to be continued, but there is also a valley temple which may have played its most important role when the king's body first arrived by river from wherever he had died. The sphinx was a part of the valley temple and was an outcropping that the king's craftsmen used to carve a likeness of him. This aspect was not standard or probably even necessary, but it is pretty impressive still, though the pollution of modern Cairo has not been kind to it.

The last of the great pyramids was built by Menkaure (meaning "Established is the soul of the Sun-God") and it too has traces of tomb and valley temples; it also has three smaller pyramids, presumably for the wives of the king. Does that mean his women were more important to him than the earlier kings' wives had been to them? Not necessarily; as we said, the Egyptians were playing it all by ear, and personal eccentricities were accommodated. Another important aspect of Menkaure's tomb you cannot see by looking at it, but texts show that the pious endowment set up for its maintenance actually did last a thousand years. And long after the king was dead and gone, there were paid priests who supplied his needs.

But why did kings of Egypt stop building pyramids? They did not really, but the resources at their command were less, and so the structures they built were less impressive. Even in the Old Kingdom there were also other styles of tombs being experimented with. The pyramids continue to be a symbol of Egypt, and for many centuries they were the largest things any humans had ever built. Later kings definitely knew that the kings of old had been more wealthy and luckier than they, and in spite of the stories Herodotus told about Khufu being a wretched tyrant, later kings of Egypt wanted to be like the Old Kingdom kings, whose glory was obvious every morning.

Inscriptions have been found in the pyramids, and in many *mastaba*s, but all the pyramids were robbed in antiquity and were found empty by modern explorers. This fact indicates that ancient Egyptians did not take the preparations for death of their rulers so seriously as the rulers or the surviving texts did. Grave robbers recycled the gold and precious objects and probably rationalized that the kings would be all right without them; better that the living have use of these things. Thieves were harshly punished if caught, but that did not stop them from trying.

Since tombs were not so important to Mesopotamians, the tombs we find are not themselves important structures. The so-called royal tombs at the southern port city of Ur were elaborate, and the person buried was a princess or queen and not a ruler herself. Down the ages we do find some royal burials especially which are rich in gold and other imports, but a good tomb was not usually on the wish list of later Mesopotamian kings.

Mesopotamian rulers boasted of their efforts in working on temples, and these mud brick buildings needed very frequent rebuildings, probably because any rain at all could damage them, and mud brick is never very stable, even if you smear it with mud or plaster to face the power of the rain. From later periods we know that rulers were careful to show respect to older versions of temples which lay underneath them, and sometimes they buried foundation deposits to assure that subsequent rebuilders would know exactly what temple they were working on.

Temple towers were an extension of temple building and restoration. They were themselves tremendous undertakings which necessitated the molding of millions of mud bricks and then their assembly into lumpy towers with steps. The idea was to build a small temple on top and to worship the god of the city in that exalted place. Herodotus, much later, had the story that these towers were used also for a sacred marriage between a priestess and a god, with the king playing the god, but the evidence for sacred marriages is slight. And because of erosion none of the several preserved temple towers has any trace of a temple on top.

Mesopotamians called the towers ziggurats, from an Akkadian word meaning "to stand straight up." The earliest and best preserved ziggurat is at the city of Ur in the far south, which more recent rulers had rebuilt. But there were other ziggurats on the Mesopotamian plain, showing the surpluses in workers and food that kings could use for such work. They are very impressive achievements, but they are not preserved as well as the pyramids, and they were never so tall. The tallest was 46 meters or 150 feet while the great pyramid is 147 meters or 481 feet tall. They contribute something to the Biblical story of the Tower of Babel which gives an origin for the multiplicity of languages people speak (Genesis 11). That story implies the tower was unfinished, and so whoever devised it may have seen the ziggurats in decay, even as we do.

These enormous buildings, the ziggurats and the pyramids, showed more clearly than anything the great power and complexity of these societies. They were monuments commemorating the kings who made them, perhaps more egotistically in Egypt than in

Mesopotamia, but in both places kings definitely wanted to take credit for all this work their people had done for them. The people themselves may have regarded much of this work as just another tedious aspect of forced labor, where they had to pay with their time instead of with their goods for the benefit of government. But from Egyptian pyramids we have some graffiti that show that the people who hefted the great stones for the pyramids were not unhappy in what they were doing. They definitely were not slaves, who were few in the Old Kingdom anyway, but perhaps many were skilled laborers, some of whom were literate. Among the graffiti is one marking a block as under the responsibilities of "the friends of Khufu," and on another pyramid there is one of "the drinking buddies of Sneferu." The attitudes of the Mesopotamians involved in temple and tower building are less clear; maybe they too knew when it was all over that they had helped with a monument that would prove to be truly lasting.

ROYAL IDEOLOGIES—GODS OR NOT

The Egyptian king came to be called "the good god," the god who was available here on earth and who might intervene on behalf of his people in their problems. This did not imply that most other gods were not good or benevolent, but they might be great gods, and so they could be busy with all sorts of other things beyond the ken of their human subjects. When modern scholars figured out what the Egyptians were saying about their kings, they assumed that this claim of deification was another instance of monomania and despotism, of overweening pride taken to ridiculous extents.

But the basic question may be what was a god in Egyptian thought. Gods included superhuman beings with more than regional power but also beings that might be honored only in one place. They might include spirits and demons of a lesser nature. We are affected by the exalted ideas of God in monotheism, and so it seems impossibly prideful to assert you are a god, with one exception, in the incarnation of Christ. And yet in the ancient world there was probably more of a continuum of uncanny and inexplicable beings, and the king's divinity could fit right in. The king's tomb was raided sometimes, and his pretensions were attacked, but denying his divinity seems not to have occurred to critics, again perhaps because it did not mean so much as it does to us.

In Mesopotamia there may have been more ambivalence about the claim to divinity, and it certainly was not so old or so prominent. The Ur III king Amar-Suen actually had a temple rededicated to him as a god while he was alive, around 2030 BCE. But when he died the place was rededicated to the local deity it had served before. Does this mean people resented the king's assumption of the temple, or did they all the time see the king as merely a manifestation of the benevolence of their local god? Maybe a little of both.

The use of the sign for god before kings' names continued into the second millennium, but we do not know if anyone pronounced it or took it too seriously. Mesopotamian kings were extraordinary in their geographic range of influence when times were good and extraordinary in the depth of tradition on which they could draw when times were not so good. Deified kings' names sometimes crop up in the names of other people, but this happens also under Hammurapi of Babylon who did not use the divine determinative. These people may have been named after the king in a bid to curry favor with the king's minions, or their parents may simply have followed the style at the time.

THE STATE AS PROTECTOR OF THE POOR—LEGISLATING MORALITY

We begin to see from texts in the late third millennium the worry kings had about their societies. We know they did not have any economic data to speak of and probably reacted to the crises that were brought to their attention on the basis of what had been common in their traditions and what seemed reasonable at the time.

There had developed an idea that the ruler should have a policy to deal with broad social problems; he usually had many more resources than other rich people and was expected to use them for the general good. This idea is derived from the roles of temples in earlier times, and the king in Mesopotamia, as in Egypt, had taken control of temples and also taken over some of their responsibilities for the poor and outcast.

In the earliest political statements, though, we do not see a religious motivation. In taking over neighboring towns, a ruler of Lagash states simply, "I established their freedom." The freedom might mean a return to an earlier situation. The word in Sumerian etymologically means "return to mother," with the warm and cozy thoughts that phrase might inspire. The king did not define what that freedom meant, and the people for whom he had established it might not have seen it in so positive a light as he and his scribes did.

A later king of Lagash, Uru-KA-gina (the capital letters mean we do not know how he might have pronounced the sign with which he wrote his name), issued a series of inscriptions that speak to similar concerns, but he was fighting that losing war with Lugalzagesi noted before. Uru-KA-gina claimed that he was giving back the temples that had previously been appropriated by his predecessors. But he did not withdraw his own family from administrative positions in the temples. He also wrote that he was restoring the old ways of taxation and withdrawing oppressive tax collectors. He said that he forbad plural marriages; this section sounds as though he was saying that women had had in the past more than one husband, but it might have meant that men had many wives. Or he might have meant that he did not want to encourage divorce and remarriage.

Uru-KA-gina was making a bid for political support for his ongoing war against Umma and trying to appeal to people who had been harmed by tax practices and who felt that the temples were no longer administering their charitable giving as they should. We see from his efforts that people in southern Mesopotamia expected kings to be concerned with justice, even in areas where they might not have had any direct control, as in marriage customs. In promulgating these statements Uru-KA-gina was trying to show that he was a concerned and engaged ruler whose views conformed with those of his people. This did not mean that he had any clear way of enforcing his views. He could have imposed new rules for tax collectors, but the change in temple administration may have been only nominal.

Uru-KA-gina lost his war and his plea for local support, and later people did not refer to his texts. But we place his work at the beginning of a long Mesopotamian tradition of issuing royal statements in support of particular social customs. The political situation of later kings who made these statements was not usually as precarious as Uru-KA-gina's. Some of them, like Hammurapi, king of Babylon, were in very strong positions internally and internationally. But the propagandistic purpose of the documents was explicit.

Hammurapi's so-called code was not the earliest nor was it the last; it was simply the longest we have preserved, and it lets us look into this royal tradition at several periods and see also how it was adapted in the Hebrew Bible, the Christian Old Testament, in the first millennium. To a large extent the point of these texts, beyond propaganda, was as teaching documents, to convey ideas of justice to new generations of scribes. We have copies of parts of Hammurapi's text from much later, indicating that scribes were still studying it as a model of legal language and of just decisions. These goals are even clearer in the Hebrew Bible legal material where later texts bristle with explanations about why we do things a certain way, the so-called motive clauses.

So were these lawgivers legislating morality? They were reflecting the ideas about what justice was current in their communities, and they did not hesitate to venture into many areas of endeavor, of family law, revenge, and economic practice. They certainly felt free to discuss morality, but as for legislating it, we are not so sure. Mostly in the ancient world we have societies that did not have police forces dedicated to regulating civilian affairs. And so the mechanism for enforcing even important royal political decisions was sketchy. Kings might decree some matters, but their influence on murder trials and marriage customs was minimal. It takes a modern state really to get into people's bedrooms and boardrooms.

3

THE SECOND MILLENNIUM: FOREIGNERS AND NEW ORDERS

The Amorites, "the Westerners," from the west of the Mesopotamian plain, had been seen as partly alien foreigners and partly usefully aggressive generals under the Ur kings. They stayed around and became the leaders of practically every state in the second millennium. They worked their way into power by becoming indispensable military leaders and then replacing the kings of the old orders. These transitions were traumatic to some of the leading personalities of Ur, and yet in many ways there was considerable continuity between the administration and even the aspirations of the ruling classes.

The Amorites were from the West, meaning Syria and Palestine, and they spoke a Semitic language related to Akkadian and later surviving languages like Arabic and Hebrew. Perhaps they came like the Arabs from the desert of northern Arabia. Their language was never written for itself, only their names in cuneiform, and we have no literature at all from them. Their names persisted over many generations, though, meaning that their language did too.

Scribes not only continued producing economic texts in much the same fashion as they had before, they also wrote down the royal hymns which had become popular with kings in the late third millennium and kept doing so for the Amorite kings. The problem with those kings was that there were so many of them, and none of them was much more powerful than any other. Control of the religious capital of Nippur in central Iraq gave the controlling king the honor of having hymns written for him and perhaps also the dubious honor of being deified.

As part of the Hyksos, the "rulers of foreign lands" who were responsible for the Second Intermediate Period in Egypt, the Amorites were involved in a different kind of intervention in Egypt. There the presence of the foreigners, though usually welcomed, in their case was not. The kings were remembered as particularly brutal. The Hyksos were depicted as evil invaders who had to be thrown out, and the fear of their reintervention may have had a role in inspiring the New Kingdom kings to invade Syria themselves and to spread the limits of Egyptian influence even to the Euphrates and up the Nile into Nubia.

Why the different reception in Egypt and Mesopotamia? We do not know. It certainly did not have much to do with the attitudes of the rulers themselves. Perhaps in Mesopotamia people were simply tired of disruption and chaos and hoped for a restoration of trade and agriculture by any means possible, and the Amorites seemed a likely bet. For centuries the little kingdoms they established were at odds with each other, and it was only Hammurapi of the small state of Babylon who managed to play the multi-party politics game well enough to get enough troops to smash his rivals, first Larsa in the south and then Mari in the northwest. His area of rule was almost as large as that of the Ur III kings, but unlike them, his family did not retain all the area, and the little empire he had made began to break apart under his son.

Hammurapi's reign was fondly remembered, however, by later Mesopotamians and also now since his Akkadian language is clear and direct and relatively easy to read. He is famous for the legacy of his collection of so-called laws. There are several lines of evidence for the idea that they were instead resolutions of the community that embodied values but were not invoked in courts. The stipulations did sometimes parallel the practice of courts, but not always and everywhere. Courts seem to have been local meetings of worthies and witnesses who met when needed and dispensed justice according to local customs.

When modern scholars first found the so-called Code in 1901 in Susa, Iran, where it had been dragged by a later king as part of his booty, they assumed it was a compilation of laws, and so a code in the modern sense, meant to be enforced. Or perhaps it was an effort to regularize customs across the broad swatch of the Iraqi plain which the king only recently had come to govern. But the code was probably not a code, and the laws were not laws in the modern sense of dictates laid down by a properly constituted authority and meant to be enforced in a jurisdiction.

The prologue to the text and its epilogue explain that it was a collection of "just judgments" that was supposed to be consulted not by courts and judges but by people with complaints who were unclear on whether they were justified in pursuing their claims. And there are few cases that involve the king or the palace; they seem to be collected judgments which groups of judges may have derived from their sense of what was just, along with others that derived logically from those practices. If a house fell on somebody, the builder was to be killed; what if it fell on some free man's slave? Right, the builder had to replace the slave.

Whether these cases ever occurred in reality was less important than the kind of justice that was being described. This justice was consistent with what might be called informal resolutions of the community which were never promulgated but frequently practiced. Courts usually had no business with murder and mayhem because these were viewed as private wrongs that had to be negotiated between families. Most preserved court cases in ancient Mesopotamia were disputes about land ownership. But Hammurapi had things to say about a wide range of practices, most of which a king could have almost no influence over.

The key concern for the king or his scribes was the preservation of property and rights to it, especially his own, but also rights to land belonging to others who had less power and influence. The text showed temporary forced labor was owed by many people and must still have been a basic way of getting large projects of irrigation and defense accomplished.

But also in Hammurapi's legal collection were listed many prices and wages, and the point was to assert that things were relatively cheap and people were getting a fair wage. Such lists were never invoked in contracts, and the prices seem unusually low in contrast to documents of sale. This underlines the idea that this text was intended as a royal inscription that described the many successes of the king. Other royal inscriptions with price lists always exaggerate how low the prices were in contrast to the documents, and such texts were not intended to be real economic indicators. Rather, they were indicators of successful reigns hoped for if not achieved.

Our division of the text into 282 paragraphs is modern and may not reflect ancient thinking about how the instances related to each other. The concerns examined are wide-ranging. Here we have murders avenged and judges who cheated. And then there is the problem which we see in earlier collections too of the marriage proposal that does not work out. In the earliest version the money that changed hands was to be given back. Hammurapi's scribes went further; if the engagement is off because a friend of the almost-groom was criticizing him to the bride and her father, then that friend could not himself marry her. Though there were probably many failed marriage proposals, these variations seem to be more of a scholarly exercise in possibilities, rather than helpful hints to marital bliss.

Another classic problem was that of the goring ox. Hammurapi says that if no one knew the ox was a gorer, then there was no liability, but if the owner did know, then he owed monetary compensation for a slave, and more for a free person, who suffered or died. Famously Hammurapi prescribed an eye for an eye and tooth for tooth; this approach seems barbaric, and yet it may be that he and his scribes were trying to guarantee that in cases involving bodily harm rich people could not simply buy their way out of the problems but would have to suffer physically.

The goring ox problem was taken up in the earliest legal collection in the Bible in Exodus 21:28–32, with the interesting twist that the ox was supposed to be destroyed if it was involved in the death of a person. This feature would have seemed odd to Hammurapi, who would have wanted to preserve the ox as a valuable farm animal, the tractor of his day. But modern scholars have suggested that Israelite horror at the violation of life demanded the destruction of the offending being, even if the animal could not be assumed to have rational control over what it did. This is the origin of the idea of the deodand in English Common Law, the principle that something involved in a crime immediately belongs to the state. Victims' compensation commissions buy back stolen cars used in robberies, for example, but the principle of sovereign power over things used in crime has not been undermined in modern times.

Though Mesopotamians did not like to generalize or speak about general principles, in Hammurapi's prologue he did state that one of his goals was to make society function so that "the strong would not oppress the weak." The weak sometimes were the abject poor, the widow and the orphan left without any clear protector. Other times in his promulgation he focused on palace dependents who might be taken advantage of by their bosses; Hammurapi wanted to ensure that such people were not deprived of their land and livelihood, and he wanted to punish those who oppressed them. In this area the king would have had some power to enforce his views.

As Hammurapi's state deteriorated, the little states around Babylon fell prey to various forces from the east and the west, and other ethnic groups came to the fore. The Kassites, who may have originated in central Syria, edged down the Euphrates and took possession of Babylon itself.

Their dynasty lasted the longest of any single Mesopotamian group, but it was preceded by a dark age. First, there was a daring raid by the Hittites of faraway central Turkey down the Euphrates to Babylon. The Hittites took booty but did not stay, and the Kassites emerged as rulers. But how long that took is not known. Various systems of getting over this dark age have proved unsatisfactory, and so the arbitrary Middle Chronology continues to be used, though the arguments for a shorter dark age are strong. Consequently all dates before the second half of the second millennium BCE may be off by 50 to 150 years.

The Kassites lasted from perhaps 1550 down to 1054 BCE, in itself a magnificent achievement. And they left hundreds of economic texts and many fewer royal inscriptions, even fewer literary texts. Theirs was a time of demographic decline; fewer people lived on fewer sites in central and southern Iraq.

To the east the Elamites reached a highpoint of complexity, and the Hittites continued to be influential in northern Syria. Directly to the north the Kassites had to interact with the Assyrians, who spoke a dialect of Akkadian and exuded a warlike pride that exulted in expansion especially toward the south and west. Part of the reason for that expansion was that northern Iraq relied on rainfall agriculture, not irrigation, and that was inherently less efficient. They may have had an expanding population and so depended on raiding to supplement their own food supply. The Kassites opposed them when they could, and that was frequently, but the Kassites did not boast of their military successes but rather of their pious efforts to rebuild temples.

The typical object of the Kassite period was the monumental text called the *kudurru*. This meant "boundary marker," but the texts were put in temples, not in fields. They recorded grants of lands by Kassite kings to people who had served them. The period has been characterized as analogous to European feudalism because of these grants, but that analogy seems misguided. The grantees did not necessarily have perpetual rights to those lands, and they did not have judicial responsibilities for them, as European nobles might.

The boundary stones implied that fewer Mesopotamians could read. The stones were rich with decorations, mostly symbols of gods meant to guarantee the land grant and to threaten anyone who might dispute the grant or otherwise bother the owner.

These kings of Babylon must have been able to convince the peasants who labored to pay their taxes that the investments they made were worth it. And they protected the central lands from the foreign invasion that could disrupt the irrigation system and devastate the villages, not to speak of the cities.

Scribal activity under the kings, whom we term Middle Babylonian, may have been considerable. Evidence for it is limited to the archival texts that record rations for laborers and temple workers from several sites; Mesopotamian meticulousness persisted. And yet interesting things might also have been happening in the area of texts that we regard as literature, which were used for advanced scribal training. There are not many literary texts preserved from the period, but there is a significant development that ought not to be underestimated. Before the Kassite period there is no clear evidence of scribes putting together even quite similar tablets into extended collections. Those were called "work assignments" or "series," *iškāru* in the Akkadian language. But after the period we have found many such collections. And in much later texts that purport to record the authors of literary compositions, the names were the long prayer-names that became popular in the Kassite period.

The kings were meshed in a big and complex world, and they knew it, thanks not only to their contacts with the Assyrians in the north but also to their links to Egypt. We know about these through the preservation of the letters from Amarna in Egypt. These are an archive of letters received by the Egyptian kings during two reigns around 1350 BCE. Letters in the ancient world were undated, and so it is not easy for us to put them in chronological order. They were written on clay in an Akkadian that reflected local dialects spoken by the scribes in different places.

The Babylonians were far from the dominant force they might once have been. Instead, they were petitioners to the kings of Egypt, like so many others, who hoped for some of the wealth of sub-Saharan Africa like gold and spices. They were also interested in making marriage alliances with the Egyptians, and this almost always meant that foreign princesses would be shipped off to Egypt for the pleasure of her kings. Egyptian princesses did not get sent abroad.

The kings of Egypt were begged similarly by kings from most of the rest of the Near East, including the Hittites in what is now Turkey, and princelings up and down the Syrian coast. Modern scholars have thought that the Egyptians were neglecting these areas, but we do not have the Egyptian replies, and so we do not know what the responses were to the letters. The kings of small kingdoms looked to Egyptian military power to solve their problems with dissident elements, and the Egyptian kings did not respond quickly enough to meet the small kings' desires.

This is the period when the Egyptian New Kingdom flourished and left us with a wealth of documentation not known earlier from Egypt. The kings, rising again from upcountry to drive out the "Shepherd Kings," as the Hyksos were translated in later traditions in Greek, established a state that was outward-looking, interested again in sub-Saharan Africa and especially in Syria-Palestine, from where the foreign kings had come.

Those Hyksos were not of only one linguistic group; some of them had Amorite names, as we have said, and so may have been distantly related to the people who took over Mesopotamia at about the same time. They presented themselves in their Egyptian inscriptions as typical Egyptian kings, but they may have ruled only the eastern part of the Nile Delta and did not get along with the worthies upriver. The Hyksos were long remembered as barbarous rulers who could not be regarded as Egyptians.

The kings who succeeded the Hyksos were from Thebes, and there they embellished a local shrine and turned it into a national center for the worship of the god Amun, the "Hidden" god who was credited with creation. The kings commemorated their martial victories there and in their elaborate columned halls memorialized their successes. This temple, now called Karnak after the modern village, became something like a Westminster Abbey, where each king felt he had to contribute some memorable monument.

We call the period also the Empire Period because of the Egyptian engagement in foreign parts. But there is some question as to whether the terminology is correct. In some places there were permanent Egyptian garrisons, and there were probably trade delegations, most famously to Punt in sub-Saharan Africa, bringing back gold, spices, elephant tusks, and midgets too. But, as we see in the Amarna letters, there were not many Egyptian governors, and the local ruling groups were left in power as long as they cooperated with the Egyptians.

The dangers the Egyptians faced included disruption of trade and also the competition from the Hittites in the far north for control of the Syrian coast and the resources inland. This competition culminated in 1274 BCE in the Battle of Kadesh, now in Lebanon on the Orontes River, the modern al-Asi River.

Kadesh was a Hittite base, and Ramses II had marched his armies deep into Lebanon to attack it, but he had to march through tortuous mountain passes. The story we have is his, and the king emphasized his own daring in leading his men into the most dangerous defiles, while others took other canyons. But as he emerged, he was surprised to be assaulted by hundreds of Hittite charioteers. He boasted that he stood alone against them and killed many until he was relieved by his own guard only at the last moment.

The battle was probably a draw. The Hittites did not lose their base, and the Egyptians withdrew. Within a few years negotiations resulted in a treaty, which we have in both a version for the Egyptians and one for the Hittites. It established a border to their spheres of influence in Syria-Lebanon and promised continuing peace between the powers. Later the Egyptian king accepted a Hittite princess in marriage, and trade connections continued.

Ramses II was among the longest-reigning kings of the ancient world, lasting sixty-seven years on the throne, and he took advantage of his long life and prosperity to build on a scale not seen earlier. Temples to him and his successes ranged from far upriver at a place called Abu Simbel down to monuments in the Delta of the

Nile. He had many wives and children and outlived several of the possible heirs to the throne.

The New Kingdom kings presided over unprecedented economic prosperity because of trade contacts and the productivity of the Nile Valley. They had figured out that pyramids were obvious and tended to be robbed of their grave goods. So they tried the caves, which, as it turned out, did not work that well either. Ramses II burrowed his tomb into the hills across from Thebes in the Valley of the Kings. It was robbed in antiquity and was denuded of its mobile treasures, but the paintings within it still amaze with their vibrant colors.

The kings set up a village of artists near the Valley of the Kings; these people did not have to work in agriculture but just prepared tombs. They were supported by the government with food and goods, and their movements may have been restricted so they could not leak any of the details of what they were working on. Many were literate and have left records of their work and of their strifes among themselves about who was being paid for what and who was sleeping with whose wife. Their own tombs could be lively creations too, showing the latest styles of painting. But when the food did not come from across the river, they were not above striking for redress of their grievances, and they were rewarded with success in their work actions. The kings and queens needed their skills.

When we try to hear voices from the New Kingdom, and we search the preserved texts, we are rewarded with a wider range of materials that were copied than in earlier times. We have some usual tomb texts which were spells people were supposed to say for their dead relatives to help them across into the blessed West. The basic idea was that the sun daily set in that direction and yet came back with no problem the next morning, and people should be able to do that too. But you needed to say the right words and provide the proper foods and drinks, or at least pictures of them, to supply the dead in their journey.

Besides those texts, which we call The Book of the Dead, we also find laments over the dead written for individuals, including several for women lamenting their husbands. These seem to be in a less formal language than other compositions and may show some of the real emotions they felt. The rites might be regarded as effective, and the blessed dead were really blessed, but such texts show that Egyptians frankly missed their departed ones, and religious ideas did not fill that loss.

Another voice of considerable interest is that of an early New Kingdom ruler who was a woman. She was the widow of Amunhotep II, whose heir was to be Thutmosis III, who had been born to another of the king's wives. The lad was probably a minor when his father died, and so Hatshepsut stepped in as regent. This was a role that had been fulfilled in earlier times by other ruling queens, but Hatshepsut took it further than ever. She had herself depicted as a king, complete with a fake beard and in breastless bare-chestedness. But she did not lie to anyone about her gender, which was obvious in nearly every sentence thanks to the rules of Egyptian grammar.

While she ruled, Thutmosis III acquiesced in what she did, and the rule lasted about twenty-one years. Then Hatshepsut disappeared, as did her only known child, a girl. Later some of her monuments were defaced, but we do not know if this was Thutmosis' idea or some program of a later king. Her huge funeral temple still stands across from Karnak and commemorates her successes at sponsoring long-distance trade with sub-Saharan Africa. She had reason to be proud of her work.

Another memorable voice is that of one of the kings to whom many of the Amarna letters were addressed, who began his reign as Amunhotep IV around 1350 BCE. Alone among the ancient Egyptians of whom we know, he wanted to reform aspects of traditional religion. He focused on a god who had been honored earlier but who may have been intended by him to rival all the others, Aten, the rim of the sun, and not the sun itself.

Amunhotep IV changed his name in his seventh year to honor that god, and he became Akhenaten, meaning "the effective spirit of Aten." He tried to suppress temples to all other gods and confiscated the many farms and goods that had been dedicated over the centuries to them. He may not exactly have been a monotheist since he held that he himself was a mediating god between his people and Aten. He broke precedent in having his family portrayed in monuments, and he himself was depicted with a paunch and a droopy, androgynous look. Though there has been much speculation about these styles of depiction, we do not know what they mean, though they certainly were new.

Akhenaten died a natural death and may not have faced much opposition to his reform efforts during his life. One of his sons, Tutankhamun, however, reverted to the more traditional religious ways of looking at things. You can see it in his name, which was changed from one meaning "living image of Aten" to the one we use now that meant "living image of Amun," the old god of Karnak. King Tut is not famous because of a long or glorious reign; he seems to have died of an infection at about the age of eighteen. But his obscure grave was only lightly disturbed by tomb robbers and discovered in the early 1920s CE, revealing opulent things, including several dismantled chariots that had been buried with him. If his grave was so rich, how much richer must have been the burials of longer-reigning and more important kings?

THE HITTITE SOLAR SYSTEM

Our first historical glimpse of what is now central Turkey is through the eyes of merchants from the northern Iraqi city of Assur. They came across the mountains to trade with the locals bringing woolen goods and also tin, from nobody knows exactly where. That metal was needed to craft local copper into bronze, the strong alloy that made the snazziest weapons in the early second millennium.

These merchants left detailed records of their caravans and their enormous profits, packed down into Mesopotamia in the form of gold. The locals they dealt with at first had names that indicate they were speaking a language we now call Hattic, which was unrelated to any other. The merchants worked in Anatolia, as Greeks later called it, for about five generations. They witnessed the arrival of a new language group, the Hittites. These people established themselves as rulers over the Hattic people and were hospitable to the Assyrians, who, however, stopped their trading sometime around 1800 BCE.

The Hittites spoke an Indo-European language distantly related to English and the languages of Europe, Iran, and India. Building a capital on the bend of the Kızılırmak, or Red River, in central Anatolia called Hattusa, they learned to use cuneiform on raids into Syria from scribes there. Their kings, addressed formally as "My Sun-god," strived to dominate Turkey and raided as far as Babylon, which they destroyed around 1600 BCE. But they did not stay in Mesopotamia.

The king who raided Babylon was murdered on his return, and the Hittite kingdom remained for generations only a local power. But about 1350 BCE these kings again began to raid south of the Taurus Mountains and built a sphere of influence that pushed against that of the Mitannians in central Syria and the Assyrians in northern Iraq. Eventually also they were in contact with the areas the Egyptians tried to control.

We would not know much about these things except that the Hittites continued to keep and to compose texts, not just in Sumerian and Akkadian, but, using the same cuneiform system, also in their own language. These texts reflected their unique heritage and were outside the usual cuneiform material.

One set of texts, King Mursili II's Plague Prayers, recorded a series of questions to the gods about why a plague was persisting in the Hittite lands. The king thought the disease had arrived with Egyptian prisoners, but he was looking for a theological and moral cause for its vehemence. His omens finally guided him to the fact that offerings to the Euphrates River had been neglected for years. The auguries also said his father had broken his oath twice. The king performed the sacrifices and tried to assuage the offended gods of the oath too. And guess what, the plague abated. But he also made sure that future kings confronted with a similar problem had access to his efforts by having the texts copied down.

Another text from an earlier period, the Edict of King Telepinu, reacted to the bloodbath of succession crises that preceded his reign and laid down clear rules which limited the people who could be Great King to descendants of the prior king; no brothers-in-law or uncles need apply. In practice his edict was ignored, but it offered a way to solve the problem of legitimate succession in an authoritarian system.

The Apology of Hattusili was a reaction to Telepinu's Edict and to traditional succession, since Hattusili III was an uncle of the previous king, whom he had deposed. This was when the Hittites had clashed with the New Kingdom Egyptians at Kadesh. The resulting treaty promised that both sides would return political fugitives who fled to them. But this did not happen when Hattusili's nephew fled to Egypt. Hattusili admitted that he had pushed the nephew out. The new king was trying to show that his nephew had been irresponsible as king and he had insulted his uncle. The interest in the text comes from Hattusili's candor and his exposure of the real problems of succession. His audience must have been not just his gods but public opinion among the Hittite elite, who remembered that in taking over Hattusili was violating earlier custom.

The overwhelming majority of texts in Hittite, preserved in the royal archives, were magical spells dealing with various crises in life, from childbirth to terminal illness. There was a lot of Hattic influence on those spells, and sometimes Hattic language itself was used. There were also incantations, magical scripts to be read to the gods, in Hurrian, a language of northern Syria spoken in Anatolia too.

And there were the Hittite laws. These seem not so closely related to the Mesopotamian law traditions in that they do not comment on the problems the Mesopotamians did, and the king made decisions in them, in contrast to Mesopotamian collections. The Hittite king could exempt people from paying a share of their fines to the palace.

Within the Hittite political control was the city of Ugarit on the coast of Syria near modern Latakia. It had a writing culture from before 1400 down to 1200 BCE, and what a writing culture. In addition to the usual languages which cuneiform scribes studied, there was also experimentation with a new script written on clay tablets but with just thirty signs. The Ugaritic scribes were writing their own language, a Semitic one. The simple system had signs that looked like cuneiform, but they stood not exactly for syllables but for the significant consonants of the language plus any vowel. In cuneiform you have different signs for /ba/ /bi/ and /bu/, but in Ugaritic a sign /b/ would stand for each of those possibilities. Vowels, however, were not depicted except that there were separate signs for the glottal stop plus a vowel. Ugaritic was one of the attempts to devise a simple system of writing which we find in the Sinai Peninsula and Syria and Palestine in the second millennium.

Ugaritic had two features of interest to us. One is that some words of the language and some of the poetic clichés it used were passed down to Biblical Hebrew; though the Ugaritians certainly were not monotheists, they did stand in the same poetic tradition as Israelites. The other feature is that we know the order of the signs, and it was more or less the order familiar in Hebrew and taken up in Greek. The basis of the order is unclear, but there it is, centuries before I had to learn the ABC jingle.

The twelfth century BCE saw an outside incursion that upset all the states of the Ancient Near East, and we can say the second millennium ended with the invasions of the Sea Peoples. These came from the Aegean area, and they were not just a raid but an invasion; they brought their families with them and were apparently trying to escape a drier climate in their own areas. They provoked a crisis that may have lasted a hundred years and diminished the power of all kings in the area.

The Egyptians successfully repulsed them twice, and they must have made some sort of accommodation with them because they hired some of them, the later Philistines, to be border guards. We find them on the Syro-Palestinian coast on what is now the Gaza Strip and also inland on the Jordan River. These people assimilated to the local surrounding populations, at least in that they abandoned their foreign pottery styles.

Farther north these movements from the sea toppled the Hittite protectorate in Ugarit on the Syrian coast, and the Hittites too stopped functioning as an imperial power. Even their capital was abandoned, and though some groups of Hittites moved south even into Syria, the states they governed were much smaller than the second-millennium one.

In the east the Assyrians were not directly affected by the Sea Peoples, but their power too diminished under pressure from tribal groups called Aramaeans. These people may have emerged from the Arabian desert in the late second millennium, and they never created a unified state. But their language eventually became the dominant one of the Ancient Near East, and their presence and perhaps their elusiveness to taxation and conscription tested the Assyrian state. Assyrians continued as a separate entity, but they lost any influence they had had in the West.

In the far south of Iraq the Kassites, who had been in dynastic alliances with the Assyrians, were finally pushed out by Elamites from Iran. There were still rulers who wanted to be considered kings of Babylon, but for a couple of centuries they were not powerful. Southern Iraq and Egypt continued to be fantastically productive in agriculture, and it may be from around 1100 BCE that the long-term population increase began which persisted into the first millennium CE.

In Syria-Palestine several little states emerged from the shake-up which the Sea Peoples and the Aramaeans had accomplished. Of these the most interesting for subsequent periods was the state of Israel. There is little archaeology from the time. The Book of Judges in the Bible, copied through centuries and reaching us as a canonical book only in the first millennium CE, presents a picture of tribally organized peoples being pressured from more politically sophisticated neighbors, like the Philistines, into creating a state.

The Biblical traditions present those kings as influential in the Aramaean-dominated world of small states, allies of the coastal Phoenicians, and consumers of the spices and gold from distant Yemen, or Sheba in the Bible. The kings David and Solomon successfully wheeled and dealt in the new Ancient Near Eastern world, Solomon even netting an Egyptian princess as a wife—an unprecedented deal from the Egyptian point of view.

In the Bible religious developments in Israel are all depicted with later teachings in mind. It seems nonetheless likely that the complex polytheism of the earlier millennia was being simplified by some elite thinkers into a devotion to one god, and then later into a denial that other gods even existed. Polytheism itself is a relatively rare phenomenon in human history and should be distinguished from animism. Animism holds that each natural thing may have a spirit which has power and may need to be bought off. Polytheism in contrast posits the existence of several independent gods who may not be related to particular things or places, but the key aspect of the gods is that they are endowed with separate and recognizable personalities. Polytheism is correlated with the existence of complex agricultural systems. It is the bedrock from which monotheism can emerge, though monotheism may only have developed once in human history, among the Israelites.

THE KING AS RAINMAKER, THE KING AS HUMAN

Because writing was limited almost exclusively to the people around the kings, we learn more about their roles, duties, and attitudes than about any other group of people in the Ancient Near East. Kings appear to have felt that the burden of success in their societies was borne by themselves. If the Nile flood failed, if rains did not come, the gods could be applied to, and the king should do it. And if he failed to figure out how to stop epidemics, people might demand another king.

We still impute to our leaders control over aspects of our lives over which they really have little control. Presidents and Prime Ministers may rise and fall on unemployment rates and debt crises, and yet most of them have been trying to do the right things for their people, given their own perceptions and ideologies. The kings of the Ancient Near East had much less good data from which to work, but the assumptions about them seem to have been similarly global.

We refer to this idea with the terms first noticed in sub-Saharan Africa about the responsibilities of rulers, that the king was responsible for making it rain and so was a rainmaker-king. Such a responsibility is still well beyond the power of any mortal, and yet the weather did affect people's attitudes as well as their crops, and moods might well affect how the political situation was going.

Because the kings presented themselves as absolute rulers, we might imagine that we do not have access to their dealings with political problems. But there are several lines of evidence about how parts of their populations felt about them and what those responsibilities really were.

The most suggestive of these comes from the first millennium BCE in a text in which an Assyrian king reported to the city of Assur, his old capital, about a campaign into the mountains to the north of Iraq, around Lake Van in Turkey. The issue he addressed was the violation of the foreigners' religious sanctuaries, something that had not happened previously. His report, though addressed to the god of the city, was meant to be read aloud to Assyrians who were members of old military families who were wondering why the king was taking their boys up into the mountains to harass those distant places and their gods. The king's answer was that the god had ordered him to do so, but he also wanted to argue that he was careful to respect the Assyrians' religious sensitivities, even as their god was obviously beating the foreign god.

From Egypt we have the Prophecy of Neferti, a text which was written as a propaganda effort to describe the coming of the first king of the Middle Kingdom around 2000 BCE. It was set up as a prophecy to an Old Kingdom king predicting famine and desolation before the new king arrived, to be made good by that king's great energy.

Kings could not count on constant success, but their scribes did try to depict them as worthy and powerful. Like modern spin doctors, the scribes omitted defeats and colored near misses as wild successes, as we saw above with the Battle of Kadesh. This aspect of royal inscriptions, not limited to the Ancient Near East, has led us to be cynical about their claims, and yet when we try to figure out the audiences being addressed, we can sometimes see what those audiences were thought to expect and how the kings tried to fit in to their expectations.

To be an Ancient Near Eastern king was extremely hard, and yet the range of people you had to appeal to may have been much more limited than the public any modern leader must address. Few were informed, fewer were literate. And yet there was a political task to accomplish, and a chain of misfortunes could lead to dire consequences for everyone, from peasants to princes. Heavy lay the head that wore the crown, and short and brutish were the lives of most people. The king needed to be seen to be concerned, and in many cases that meant working on his reputation not for truth but for justice.

Success was in general the criterion for authority, and the success might have to be more impressive the less blazing the other contributors to authority were. No one wrote down a list of what you needed to be king, but kings liked to emphasize their characteristics in their inscriptions. Not every king could have each one, but having more was better. One characteristic was descent from an old and venerable line of kings, but we know that some actually admitted that they did not have this. One Old Babylonian king boasted that he was "chosen from out of a crowd." Accustomed to the royal houses of Europe, we assume this descent was necessary, but clearly it was not.

If you could not claim descent, you could claim relationship through marriage. This was less secure, but seems to have been tried by a variety of princes, notably Israel's King David who married Saul's daughter. Another quality would be success on the battlefield, and again many kings claimed this, though the evidence of actual royal deaths in battle after they became king is scant: Ur-Nammu of the Ur III Dynasty in southern Mesopotamia was said to have died that way, and in the first millennium King Saul and Sargon II. In most cases warriors, once they became king, preferred to have other people lead armies in the field.

If you could not look to an athletic reputation in battle, at least you could look good, and, in Saul's case, be taller than others. Most kings did not dwell on how they looked in their inscriptions, but they did have themselves depicted usually with broad shoulders and aggressive stances, models of stability and legitimacy.

Still, things could go wrong. Conspiracies against kings especially in their families brought down many a crowned head, famously in the Hittite empire. Perhaps especially in newly established kingdoms, of which we have plenty in the first millennium, there may always have been doubt about what the king's real powers were and whether he really had the right to exercise them.

You can see what the problem was, with poor roads, impassable in the winter rains, and subjects who were nomadic or potentially nomadic. You could not command them if you could not find them. You might have an impressive palace as the king of Mari had, but you still might have to keep traveling to keep the lid on everything.

The impression we get is of an uneasy crown and a difficult, if privileged, life. You might live longer and better than your subjects, but the court and your foreign enemies were eager to take your place, to tuck your hard-earned treasure in among their own, the better to bribe and reward the people through whom they passed, claiming also to be kings appointed by the gods. Religious sanction may have been helpful everywhere, but it did not stop envy and the coups.

In Egypt the king who died was identified with the king of the afterlife, *Wsjr* in Egyptian, "The Strong One," Osiris in Greek, who endured after the sun moved west, where the blessed dead lived. The succeeding, live king was said to be Horus, Egyptian *Ḥr*, perhaps "The Distant One." He was identified with the sun who moved toward the west each day. Preparations for death were elaborate, and the king's endurance depended after death on the success of his grave goods.

Mesopotamian royal burials were rarer and not so conspicuous as the pyramids. Everyone was assumed to go to a fairly rotten Hades. And yet the ruler of the Netherworld was sometimes Gilgamesh, a formerly human king of the large southern city of Uruk who had sought an eternal name, as was narrated in his epic, and had become a god, at least after death. The Ur III kings identified with him, and that may be why his story was preserved.

Again being a god had its advantages, but these did not exempt the king from worries about the weaknesses that afflict us all. And his concerns may have been heightened by the presence of that treasure and the doubtfulness of that legitimacy.

We end with a fable from the Hittite world:

> The young mother just knew the baby was sick, very sick. He would no longer take her breast but would just lie still and cry. She had already had two children die, more or less in the same way. They would stop eating, lose all their liquids to diarrhea, and finally get so weak they could not go on, and they did not.
>
> She was frantic. The baby had been perfect, born easily with little labor, and her husband had been proud to see he had a son, one who would eventually be useful in the back-breaking farm work that he was doing. And the baby's thriving meant his young wife, much younger than the husband, was capable of reproduction.
>
> Now, the husband was afraid. The young mother had no ideas, and so the husband left the village and hiked up to his mother's village. Did she have any suggestions? The grandmother fed him his favorite meal and said this happened all too often. An aunt stopped in, and the question was put to her. "I have heard of a healer," she said. "Where? Who?" the husband asked.
>
> "I can show you," the aunt said, "but she doesn't speak our language."
>
> "I speak Hurrian too," the husband boasted in Hittite.
>
> "No," the aunt said, "she speaks only Hattic," referring to the older language of Anatolia. This gave the husband pause. The Hattics were the first people here, and they knew the herbs and mosses that might help, and they knew the names of the old gods that used to haunt these places, before the Hittites even arrived.
>
> The aunt walked the husband to another village and showed him a run-down hut. It was clear from the aunt's demeanor that she was afraid of the Hattic woman.
>
> The husband ducked down to the door, knocked and entered. He could see nothing inside, so dark was the hut, but in the back there was a single candle burning, and a very old crone raised her eyes to him. He did not know what to say. He pantomimed holding a baby. The crone looked at him as if mystified, then nodded, stood up, collected a small bag that had been lying on the floor, and pushed him out the door, following him.
>
> In the wan daylight the old lady stumbled, but the husband took her arm. She seemed unused to walking anywhere, and it was quite a walk.

He pantomimed a question of whether she needed water or food. She denied she did, and they walked on slowly.

It took all day to get back to the village, and the Hattic crone would not stop. When the husband sat down to rest or drink, she pulled him up and crabbed at him in her language. He understood that there was no time to waste. His son's life might even now be ebbing away.

It was dusk as they came into his village. The husband hastened to his hut and found the mother asleep and the baby barely breathing.

The old woman insisted the young mother squirt some of her milk into a wooden cup; she would not use a pottery cup. Then she shooed the couple outside, over their protests, in a language they could not understand. The husband and wife held each other in the darkness, whispering about where he had found the old woman and what might happen now.

All the cold night they sat before the hut's door and heard only a low chanting in the foreign tongue. The couple both eventually fell into an uneasy sleep.

They were awakened by the cries of the infant, but these were not like the earlier whimpers. These were lusty cries of hunger. The young mother rushed in and found the old woman cradling the boy. The old woman smiled, and handed the lad to his mother. The infant sucked happily.

The mother thanked the old lady, who just smiled. The husband came in and got out some broken silver which he presented to the crone. She refused it; she also refused drink or food. She said something in Hattic, got up, gathered her bag and started to make her way home. She kept the husband from coming with her.

Later the husband came to know a low official at the king's court and mentioned this story to him and to a scribe who also worked there. The scribe was interested, having lost children of his own, and the husband and the scribe set off one day to find the Hattic lady to take down her remedy and her spells; they could not find her, for she had died, but they did find a daughter of hers who remembered parts of her mother's prayers, and these the scribe did take down.

Something like this happened to enrich the Hittite library, recorded in cuneiform on clay tablets, with spells that might be useful for all kinds of ailments.

THE FIRST MILLENNIUM: WORLDWIDE STATES

Another fable:

> The king was upset at the news from back home. A courier, dusty and tired, had just slid in from the north, and he smelled like the camel he had come on. He was ushered in to see the king immediately; he fell at his feet, kissed the hem of his robe, and blurted out, "The Persians are coming!"
>
> "What do you mean by that?" the king asked. "The Persians helped us rid the world of the wretched Assyrians, and we have been allies since."
>
> "No, lord," the messenger said, still with his face near the floor, "the Persians have assembled an army in their hills and are marching down into the plain with the intention of overthrowing your august leadership. They have broken all their promises."
>
> The king looked out over his newly built city in the center of Arabia, hundreds of miles from the Mesopotamian plain. His idea had been to create a new place where his religious innovations could take root. But had they? He had had to drive the Arabs who had lived there from their homes because they had refused to accept him or to realize that his devotion to the moon god was as important to him as it was to them. But they had not even wanted to hear what he had to say.

Perhaps the translator had botched things. He did not know. That had been ten years ago.

He had left his son back in Babylon, a fine young man who could become a great king, but now he faced a greater challenge than mere administration. Belshazzar said in the message, which had been memorized by the messenger, "There is unrest in the streets of Babylon. Even the priests are in rebellion."

"So there are people opposing us even in Babylon?" asked the king.

"Yes, lord. There were crowds in the street when I left," the messenger said.

The king thanked the messenger and sent him away with silver; his slaves were instructed to make sure he was well fed and housed for the night. But the king himself wandered the palace, unsure if he should immediately decamp. He had advisors around, of course, but he did not want to be troubled by their opinions this night. He merely wanted to understand what had gone wrong.

He had been so sure that his course had been correct. His mother, then alive, had encouraged him to follow his heart and do what the gods told him was the right thing to do. And she had spent her entire life in selfless devotion to the god of the moon. Where was the god tonight?

The king scanned the skies, but there was as yet no moonrise, and this disturbed him. He would have liked a nice smiling moon to look down and bless his thoughts tonight. But it was not there, at least not yet.

The people of Babylon simply did not understand what he was trying to do, to rethink the whole of Babylonian religion and acknowledge the primacy of the moon, not a new god by any means, but one that looked over humankind benignly, marking months and years, adjusting for us the seasons, giving us peaceful nights. His gifts were manifest to everyone, and yet the Babylonians did not care to understand the moon's importance.

Of course, there would always be those who worshipped the all-seeing sun, or the powers of the female, and the king would be the last person in the world to deny the importance of those elements. But still the moon ruled the night, and the night was really the decisive element with which humans had to contend. Why could the Babylonians not see that? And the grace and beauty of the moon, fully given to anyone who would look up. Perhaps that was it; the Babylonians never took the trouble to look up.

And now they were welcoming in a foreigner, a barbarian, whose religion was what? Did anybody really know? He seemed to worship some of the old gods, but really no one could tell. And they preferred that Persian to him, the native son of the river valley?

But enough of that sort of thought. Nabonidus bustled toward the office of the supervisor of his household to command him to prepare to move everyone back to Babylon, to dispute this Persian's faithless attack, to fight if need be till the end to defend his rule.

This may have been something like the meditations of the last native ruler of Mesopotamia in the autumn of 539 BCE. Nabonidus was a religious reformer, but he lacked literate supporters who could defend and perpetuate his ideas.

When we consider the first millennium BCE, we are looking backwards from about the time of the birth of Christ, and the transition to the later period did not happen exactly a thousand years before him in every place. But something was certainly happening which had not happened before.

Some people looking back at it from an archaeological point of view speak of the new period as the Iron Age on the grounds that iron, which had been known at least in Turkey in earlier periods, became more common. And yet these sorts of age distinctions were not particularly meaningful to most people since most people did not have access to the metal. Iron had its advantages over bronze, though, because it was found in lots of places and did not require the admixture of tin, which had come from the east of the Ancient Near East and was difficult to find and expensive to buy. Iron was also easy to work; it could be poured into molds and hammered into shapes, and techniques of annealing—heating and then rapidly cooling—created very hard objects which could cut through many kinds of material. But the coming of the Iron Age in one place did not mean that iron had reached others.

The Bible has the story, which is not actually supported by archaeology, that the Philistines had a monopoly on smiths, which they would not share with their enemies the Israelites (1 Samuel 13:19–22). This story implies that iron was a less democratic metal than bronze, but it became widespread and cheap. Soon it was everywhere.

THE SMALL STATES—INNOVATION BY COMBINATION

There was a proliferation of small polities in the areas that had been dominated earlier by outside forces and by powerful city states. Throughout Syria and Palestine small groups of people created new ways of ruling themselves, some of which may have been more open to the voice of the people.

Some have called these states tribally based and others have suggested ethnic states as a term. What these expressions reflect is the idea that the leaders of these polities saw themselves as linked to tribal identities. This might have involved some of the elements that later led to feelings like nationalism.

In Israel we do not initially see language as an ethnic identifier. Nobody had any trouble talking to Philistines, for example, though at an early date those people probably did speak Greek. But in the stories in the Bible we see that tribal identification had been important, even though it faded over time.

Scholars used to suppose that tribal identity meant that the group had been nomadic before, wandering about on the desert fringes of the Ancient Near East finding pasturage for animals. At first nomads followed donkeys and sheep, but in the first millennium it was camels. Camels were great because they could go farther without water and they could carry greater loads than donkeys.

But even in Israel it is not so obvious that we have stories of nomads. The founder, Abram, had big flocks and moved around a lot, but he also had slaves and even fields. The stories about the other patriarchs were also unclear about their living patterns, though they did travel long distances.

But tribal identity does not necessarily indicate a close connection with the desert. In Syria now you can meet settled farmers who farmed where they live for generations who still have tribal alliances. Some of their cousins may be nomads still, though all governments of the region want nomads to settle down because they are hard to count, to draft, and to tax. And yet the tribal identity persists.

It is possible that city living, increasingly an attractive option in the modern Middle East, slowly dilutes this sort of loyalty. In Israel the importance of tribes did gradually diminish.

At Mari in Syria there were important tribes in the second millennium, whose support was of gripping importance to the kings there. But what was happening in the first millennium seems different, as if tribal leaders themselves were forming states, bringing other tribes in to form combinations that were stronger than a single tribe would be by itself. This happened not just in Israel, but also further north, where royal inscriptions show compound states, where a single king boasted of ruling two different places he named. This probably had political meaning to his subjects; he was king not just of Hamat but of Luath too.

Perhaps because of our familiarity with the Bible we may not so clearly see that the so-called united kingdom was a union not really of twelve tribes, but of two coalitions, a northern one and a southern one. They eventually split into the kingdom of Israel and the kingdom of Judah. Both were viewed by opinion leaders as ethnically and religiously the same, but their fates were different.

What was included in the new states was flexible, and new groups could be added. The political fragmentation and combinations we see in Syria also happened in Anatolia. In Iraq and Iran these are not so clear to us, and we are best informed about the groups that continued to use cuneiform script and the Akkadian language.

The Iraqi polities included the shadowy kings of Babylon—later king lists recorded several short-lived dynasties—and also the kings of Assyria. These northern leaders presided over the rump state that had been left by the movements of groups in the late second millennium and saw themselves as heirs of a long and glorious tradition which they wanted to renew.

Egypt too was divided into small states whose leaders remembered pharaonic glory though not how to get back to it. They understood that there should be one king in Egypt, but could not agree on who that should be, and temples and priests again provided the continuity that was needed for smooth functioning of the agricultural system, always of course taking a nice cut for themselves.

Politically in this new world order it was possible for previously unknown groups to become prominent, and through trade to be influential not just in their immediate neighborhoods but sometimes far beyond. The stories of Israel are best known, involving King Solomon building a merchant fleet on the Gulf of Aqaba for trading down the Horn of Africa and to the east. The legendary visit of the queen of Sheba, from what is now Yemen, reflected these possibilities.

The Phoenicians were the most influential in trade in the long term. These people lived on the Syrian and Lebanese coast and had long been involved in trade by sea. Shipwrecks in Turkey reveal small boats laden with containers for olive oil and wine and also tin ingots. Now in the first millennium these sailors were famous for their dyes, particularly the purple that they got from sea urchins, for which the Greeks called them *phoinikes*, Phoenicians, from *phoenix*, "red or purple."

Phoenicians would not have identified themselves as an ethnicity but more likely would have referred to themselves as dwellers in particular cities, Tyrians and Sidonians. Archaeology shows that they sailed all over the Mediterranean and out into the Atlantic; they set up settlements, most of which were intended to be permanent. The famous ones that persist are Marseilles in southern France and Cadiz on the Atlantic coast of Spain, but there were many others.

Sometimes their settlements were on islands or peninsulas, like Cadiz, chosen for their easy access to the sea and for protection against the local inhabitants. But their relations with the locals needed in general to be symbiotic if trade were to happen regularly.

Their greatest impact was in how they wrote. They had inherited the experiments that had been tried in Syria in the second millennium to simplify the scripts used by the earlier scribes. The order of the signs they used was the same as that at Ugarit in northern Syria. This is the order that we still preserve as we use this system, starting with a glottal stop, the sound you make when you begin a word starting with a vowel, a slight opening at the back of the mouth, and then /b/ and /g/, followed by /d/.

The shapes of the signs chosen were derived from experiments in simplifying Egyptian hieroglyphs that showed up over the course of the previous millennium especially in the Sinai Peninsula. But they have gone their own way, and the Phoenicians had only 22 signs, in contrast to the 120 or so used in cuneiform at any one time and the 700 in Egyptian hieroglyphics.

But was this an alphabet? Not in the technical sense that there was a specific sign for every sound that made a difference in the

Phoenician language. Vowels were not indicated at all at first and only came to be shown by the use of other consonants which might be related to the vowel sounds, like /w/ for /o/ or /u/ and /h/ for /a/. Later tradition calls such letters "mothers of reading," but there was a lot of reading going on before their use as indicators of vowels.

Still, the Phoenician system was a simplification even if it only indicated consonants. Probably people who were used to using syllabaries, where each sign stood for at least two related sounds, may have thought of the Phoenician system as signs that stood for a consonant plus any vowel, as we saw in Ugaritic. For native speakers, such a system was adequate, as it still is in various English shorthand techniques.

To learn this system must not have taken much time, and it gradually increased the number of people who could read and the kinds of things that would be recorded. There was one deplorable aspect of the system, though, and that is that it was used on perishable materials much more than the earlier writing had been. And so what is preserved is the monumental inscriptions on stone and later especially grave inscriptions.

The Phoenician system was borrowed for related languages quickly, and we have Aramaic inscriptions in the system. But it was also borrowed to depict the unrelated languages of Greece. This transfer was a result of the Phoenicians' trading trips, and it may have initially been borrowed by people of low social status who had been cut out of earlier Greek-speaking high culture; hence perhaps the disdain for writing of Plato, the philosopher of the fourth century BCE. An aristocrat himself, he did not want the lower classes to have access to traditions; he wanted the leisured classes to memorize large swatches of material, probably excluding poetry, which he thought tended toward the immoral.

When the Greeks borrowed the system, they used some of the signs for the vowels that they had which were crucial in how the roots and declensions of their language worked. They ended up with the "mother of writing" for /y/ as the vowel /i/ and other signs for other vowels. They remembered in later ages where these signs came from, and the myths about the Cadmean letters show even in Cadmus' name the eastern connection; qdm meant "east" in Phoenician. This more alphabetic system was adapted by other people to the west, and it is the system in which you are now reading. It has proved itself a supple instrument that could be adapted to new languages with different sounds.

Politically the Phoenicians were organized in city states, and they did not necessarily cooperate with each other. The colonies which they flung abroad were loyal to particular cities back on the Syro-Lebanese coast. They may have served as a model for the spread of Greek colonies which started later throughout the Mediterranean, especially in southern Italy and Sicily, where several important cities were founded.

Why did people leave home in this time? Perhaps there was perceived population pressure in the older cities, or perhaps, as in later colonial movements, it was the perception, not always borne out in reality, that emigration would offer people who were not in the elite groups the possibility of making new fortunes and reaping advantages that could not be found at home. People were heading out for the territories and did not always know what they would find, but unlike in Huck Finn's time it was usually very hard to get back.

RELIGIOUS CHANGE ON THE EDGES

The first millennium was the time of origin of a number of traditions which still persist in human thought, and all of these were revisions of and rebellions against earlier ways of thinking. We are not sure why they may all have come to the fore at roughly the same time, but it could be that a more widespread literacy in many places recorded ferment which previously was there but went unrecorded.

It was in Israel where the impact was the greatest. It was a peripheral state, formed because of the pressure of the Philistines on the mountain heartland where the Israelites had formed their kingdom. When exactly the new ideas took hold in Israel is subject to dispute because all the stories about the period come from later times and were seen as charters endorsing contemporaneous power relationships and practices. Kings and temples and priests used the stories to show the antiquity and the divine authority for power. The stories could be self-serving, but the most interesting thing was that the stories were not monolithic. The Book of Leviticus might emphasize how important priests were, but Exodus 32 criticized them.

In Israel a small group of thinkers used polytheism as a base to assert the importance of a single god for the people related to them. This may have been an extension of earlier ideas about particular gods showing special concern for individual families; it does not seem to have anything much to do with nomadism or tribes since when we hear about it in detail these social aspects had faded in importance. This idea has been called henotheism, meaning that there may have been many gods, but only one was relevant for our group.

Still, the names people used show that there were several different gods dealt with in that way, the eventually dominant one having the name YHWH, in the Phoenician script without indicated vowels. This name came to be seen as the personal name of God; it was probably pronounced "Yahweh" and meant "He causes to be," a great name for a creator God. But he may not have been a creator at the beginning of Israelite thought. He dwelt upon a mountain, but he did come down to help his special people in their hours of need.

Some of the intellectuals began to assert that YHWH was "a jealous God" who did not want His people acknowledging other gods. But the key event that forged a religious breakthrough was the exile of the southern kingdom of Judah to Babylon after 597 BCE. We will see later how the event fits into imperial politics, but here the important thing is that the Judahite victims of the deportation may have been few in number and highly literate. Some, like Ezekiel, were priests, and many were steeped in their earlier traditions. They confronted in Babylon, at the time probably one of the largest cities in the world, a myriad of religious practices. The exiles may have been at first bewildered as to what to do religiously. There certainly was a strain in polytheism that said that gods were connected to particular places; if you were in a new place, you might need to worship a new god.

But some of the exiles saw such attitudes as apostasy from the early traditions and preached that the God of Israel was mobile, was still caring for His people even in distant exile. The breakthrough assertion was made by a prophet we now call the second Isaiah, second because his book was attached to that of the earlier prophet of that name. This thinker asserted that not only were Babylonian gods stupidly irrelevant; they were also non-existent. There was no other god anywhere except the God of Israel.

This is the monotheism that the three great Middle Eastern religions assert, and it raised immediately the question of what God thought about all the other people in the world and how they were to be treated by those who knew the truth. The answer was that Israel was to be "a light to the [other] nations" to explain how YHWH worked. There does not seem to have been any immediate idea of converting people or participating in missionary outreach, but those ideas were implied by Second Isaiah's views and came into focus over the centuries.

This monotheism was a simplification over polytheism, but it could not replace many of polytheism's basic assumptions, and it did not easily explain the existence of evil. In polytheism bad things happened because some god or spirit was angry; in monotheism bad things happened as a consequence of human action, but did not the only God, seen as all-powerful, foreknow and even direct all things? This problem is not soluble in monotheism, and yet monotheism has been a comfort to its adherents, who no longer needed to worry about offending the many local gods, but only the one God.

Among the other innovative religious trends of the mid-first millennium in the Ancient Near East was Zoroastrianism. Zoroaster was a prophet in Iran, whose date and message cannot be known because all texts relating to him come from very much later, and they do not refer to contemporary datable events. Perhaps he lived as early as 1000 or as late as 500 BCE. He tried to reform previous Iranian religion, a diverse polytheism like that in India, whose Indo-European languages were related to Persian.

Zoroaster taught that there was not a myriad of gods, but really only two, a great god who fought for the good, and a bad one who fought for the bad. Human beings had always to decide which side they were on. Other spirits existed too in his system, but they paled to meaninglessness next to the epic dualistic struggle. Evil could be explained in that way, and good always needed to be defended. These dualistic ideas were adopted in Judaism and Christianity and to a much lesser extent in Islam to endow evil with personality, but they always remained fringe views difficult to reconcile with the majesty of the one God.

Bearers of the great river valley traditions did not feel a need to revise their key ideas, and so the innovations that are with us still did not take hold there. Egyptian religion in this late period still was open to outside traditions, and a change involved turning to gods who were depicted as animals and away from ones that looked like human beings. In Mesopotamia the last Babylonian king, Nabonidus, may have tried to bring the worship of the moon god from the periphery of Babylonian thought to its center. But this turned out to be very unpopular with the intellectuals faithful to the older gods. They thought he was insane and wrote that he was and were happy to greet the Persian conqueror Cyrus when he came down from Iran into Iraq, as we saw in the fable at the start of this chapter.

PERILS OF EMPIRE—DEPORTATIONS AND IDENTITY

In the 880s BCE in northern Iraq a state grew out of the old city state of Assur and evolved quickly into an empire. We have seen such structures before in the Ancient Near East, systems where a conquering army imposed annual tribute on surrounding peoples in exchange for protection from others if they were threatened. It is easy to be cynical about such arrangements and to attribute them to the greed of the more powerful parties.

But as argued above, such systems do not persist without interested collaborators on the ground, especially if they attempt to be successful across great distances. Empires depend on collaborators, and the enticements to collaborate must be kept attractive and continual, including kickbacks on contracts. Allurements could consist of some of the tribute collected by the empire's bureaucrats coming back to local leaders. Sometimes the enticements can be in the form of ranks in the army or administration, preferment for the local leader's relatives or clients. Or sometimes the empire would include a collaborator's gods in a pantheon and would consult him when facing local issues.

The threat to the endurance of empires, though, is that local opinion leaders always ask what the empires have done for them lately. Empires create perpetually demanding clients in those collaborators, and the system continues to work only if the goods and intellectual benefits were felt to continue to flow.

Assyria ecologically was an odd place for an imperial center. It was on the edge of the dry-farming area, and its river, the Tigris, was a down-cutting gorge-making river which was usually difficult to tap for irrigation. It may have been this agricultural marginality that inspired early Assyrian kings to look outward for food for their people.

In the first millennium after recovering from incursions from Aramaeans the heirs of the second millennium kings began to assert themselves in this new world order which till then, about 886 BCE, had been free of great powers from any direction. But then the Assyrians began almost annual raids toward the south as far as they could go, then into the west up the Euphrates into the grain-growing belt of Syria. The Assyrians did not want to rule tribute-supplying areas directly and were ready to support whatever local worthies were available. But they did insist on delivery of farm goods after the harvest, and when they were out campaigning they also demanded that cohorts of fighting men join them as auxiliaries. These military collaborators could look forward to being fed by their Assyrian masters while in the field and also to bringing home some of the tribute collected. Their families would worry about their dying on distant battlefields, but the client leaders in their communities found such contributions worthwhile most of the time.

And so fairly quickly the Assyrian army grew to gigantic propor-tions that had no precedents. In earlier periods three thousand soldiers had been a lot, and in the Amarna letters even one or two hundred seemed to make a real difference. But the Assyrians fielded 40,000 to 50,000 at a time, and sometimes as many as 70,000. True, such a host was a nightmare to feed and a nightmare to lead. But it could be stunningly imposing. Many threatened princes either abandoned their lands entirely, the option the Assyrians would discourage since no farmers meant no food for them, or submitted as soon as the word came through that the host was on its way. If ever an Assyrian king failed to launch an annual summer campaign, though, the tribute payments fell off, and the motivation for exerting more pressure on the laggard payers was great.

The army and its campaigns were the basic mechanisms of domination, but they were not the only ones. Overland transport was the main option chosen for getting foodstuffs back to Assyria, and there were relay depots established to make sure there were donkeys and people to make the transfers happen. More ominously the Assyrians pushed the art of deportation.

Earlier kings had occasionally made people move from their homes to other areas the kings wanted populated. The motive was to break up a local political infrastructure that had fomented rebellion. The Assyrians had done this at the end of the second millennium, though the volume of deportation had never been so great as it became in the first millennium.

The Assyrians wanted to undermine the social structures by deporting opinion leaders. They deported them back to the heartland of Assyria, which Assyrians felt was underpopulated. The people exiled were not enslaved but were treated as peasant farmers who owed taxes but were relatively free in what else they did. This policy affected more than a million people over the 250 years when it was most vigorously used, in a landscape much more thinly populated than now. And the policy worked; there continued to be rebellions in the outlying places from which deportees were taken, but there were none in the Assyrian heartland.

Still, the forced uprooting of people did not endear the Assyrians to the people who left or those who remained, and when an Assyrian king died, there were rebellions against the new king. These deportations destroyed the ethnic self-consciousness of the deportees after a generation or two, except for the Judahites. They had taken counsel from the exile of their northern neighbors and kinsmen in the kingdom of Israel in 722 BCE. Some 27,290 were deported in that instance, according to the Assyrians, but Judahites took notice. This exile so alarmed people in the south that they worked on organizing their traditions including presumably their old books in such a way that when their turn came, as it did only 124 years later, people were ready to maintain their traditions in a new land. As we said above, this exile was the one that was decisive for the forging of later Judaism.

Like their armies the scope of the Assyrians' empire was unprecedented. They tried to rule the whole region from Babylonia into Egypt, which they conquered under their last important king. The logistical problems must have been daunting, and communication was slow and easily disrupted. The hostility the Assyrians had inspired almost everywhere assured that any stumble on their part would be met with rebellions.

The events at the end of the Assyrian empire are unclear, but the downfall was rooted in the plan of the next to last king to divide his realm between his two sons. After his death, this assured a civil war which weakened the empire and eventually opened it to more systematic opposition than previously had been possible.

The winners were a family of Babylonians who had come to prominence as military collaborators of the Assyrians, and they were joined by the Persians, from the Iranian plateau. The east had been ignored by most Assyrian kings, and this neglect allowed tribal leaders to forge new alliances that gave them more fighting men that could be mobilized. In the late 600s the Persians did not want to rule the Iraqi plain, and so the Neo-Babylonians took over.

The question among small kingdoms out west was whether imperial policies would be continued. The assumption of most rulers was that they would not be, but the Neo-Babylonian kings imposed their will on the western coalitions and continued Assyrian practices, from grain depots to deportations. Why this arrangement did not last was connected to the former ally, the Persians, who had slipped into control of the northern slice of the Ancient Near East. They became aware of dissent against the Neo-Babylonians and consented to topple them with the cooperation of elites in Babylon who had come to feel that Nabonidus, the last Neo-Babylonian king, had betrayed the old and revered religious traditions, as seen in the fable beginning this chapter.

Nabonidus himself was a character and a polarizing one. We learn most about him from his enemies, and he may have ended up without many friends. The moon god had been in the Mesopotamian pantheon always, but Nabonidus exalted his position. Nabonidus did not edge toward henotheism, but he was emphasizing matters which the learned elites did not like to see changed.

Not only that, but he left town for the better part of ten years, to go and live in central Arabia, of all places. The priests back in Babylon saw this as a betrayal of his proper role of "taking the hand of Bel," or Marduk, at the spring new year's festival. But Nabonidus wrote that he was worshipping the moon god in a new land. He was not there to make friends, though, since he made war on the nomads living around the oasis he chose, Teima, and there he built a Babylonian city.

We do not really understand what he may have been thinking, but he was remolding aspects of Mesopotamian religious thought. He did not have literate followers, and so his goals remain unexplained.

Perhaps he was trying for a rethinking of religious traditions on the lines of what had been happening among the Jews and the Zoroastrians, but the traditions of Mesopotamia were simply too old and too tightly held for him to make much headway. His opponents declared him insane, and the figure of the more famous king Nebuchadnezzar in the Biblical Book of Daniel owes something to this judgment. In Daniel it is Nebuchadnezzar who wandered about insanely like a beast until he was healed, saw the error of his ways, and became a monotheist. The insanity was the accusation against Nabonidus, and though he never became a monotheist, he did have new ideas repugnant to traditional religion. Nabonidus' opponents embraced the Persian king as a rational alternative.

This was in 539 BCE, and with Nabonidus' fall Iraq was to be ruled by foreigners from that time till the bloody coup of 1958 CE. The first foreign rulers were the Persians.

THE WORLDWIDE STATES—PERSIANS AND GREEKS

The Persians stormed in from the east to replace the Babylonians, and they swept into the west and down into Egypt. They retained control of Anatolia. They were trying to reestablish the Neo-Assyrian empire, but they improved on the model with some innovations which persisted whenever states tried to integrate others into a worldwide system.

We should note that we know about these innovations mostly from Greek and Jewish sources and not from the Persians' royal inscriptions, which are few and laconic. We have travelogues from Greeks who visited and worked for the Persians, and Biblical books including Ezra, Nehemiah, Daniel, and Esther are set in the Persian court or reflect Persian policy. Greeks were divided on whether Persian domination was a good thing, and they resisted it in Ionia, on the Turkish coast, and eventually united to oppose the two tries by the Persians to integrate mainland Greece into the empire. Jews regarded the empire as a benign innovation which they could support and sometimes fight for.

There is one ideological change that is explicit in the Persian inscriptions, though, and that is the idea that the myriad foreign countries had to be subdued in order to impose law and order on them.

They had been living in chaos until the Persians arrived, the Persian kings said. Another change is harder to gauge, and that is the kings' allegiance to Zoroastrianism; the symbol for the Great God floats above them on their carved rock walls, but otherwise this allegiance was not made clear in inscriptions or elsewhere. And the Persians had no intention of imposing their religious views on others.

The Biblical books of Ezra and Nehemiah say that Persians had a new religious policy which encouraged local religions and even allowed returns from exile, some of which the Persians were willing to pay for. These views were self-serving for the Jews, but they appear to have represented Persian policy, which stressed tolerance for local traditions. Among Jews and probably other groups who had been disrupted and oppressed by the Assyrians and the Babylonians this policy was popular. The prophet called the Second Isaiah even thought the conquering Persian emperor, Cyrus II, was the messiah of YHWH, meaning a leader specially appointed to carry out God's will (Isaiah 44:28, 45:1–5).

Another imperial innovation of the Persians was the roads. The Greeks spoke of the long road the Persians had put together from Sardis to Persepolis, meaning from the Turkish coast up into the Iranian highlands. It may have been not a paved or cleared route but only a series of way stations where royal messengers could change horses. Officials could get information from west to east and vice versa within seven riding days; this was as fast as lightning in the ancient world. The road also encouraged trade, and there is evidence that lots of people traveled throughout the empire, some returning to ill-remembered homes they had occupied before they or their parents were exiled, like the Jews, others to take advantage of the newly integrated economic union. For the empire meant that petty princes were not taxing traders every few miles, and imperial forces might even protect them against robbers on land and pirates marauding at sea.

Another new thing the Greeks noticed was the institution they called "the Eyes of the King." These were traveling Persian officials who kept the king aware of adverse political developments but mainly were concerned with auditing accounts of other Persian officials. The point was to reduce waste and fraud and to assure that the king got the maximum possible return from taxes.

Of course there were collaborators, especially after the first chaotic decades of the empire, when there was doubt about succession to the kingship. People in the west enjoyed the newfound freedom of movement.

Egyptians too hoped for more independence. But among the collaborators was a group of Jewish soldiers stationed down at the first waterfall on the Nile, at Elephantine Island, across from modern Aswan. They were there to keep hostile forces from sub-Saharan Africa from invading Egypt. The Jewish soldiers and their relatives left an amazing cache of contracts and letters written on papyrus in the Aramaic language and preserved because of Egypt's dry climate. They show many aspects of daily life, including the marriages and divorces of Jewish women, some of whose husbands had Egyptian names. And they also show the Jews claimed one of their Persian commanders persecuted them and burned down their temple. Another letter reveals the Jews asking authorities in Jerusalem if they could celebrate the Passover. And a list of temple contributions indicates that YHWH was worshipped along with a goddess. They called themselves Jews, but they were not entirely conforming to the idea of what Judaism would be like from the Hebrew Bible. This community disappeared eventually with the empire, but Jews continued to live and thrive in Egypt.

The Persian empire integrated many "peoples and tongues," as the Biblical Book of Esther called them. The kings were distant figures, and their officials were frequently not Persians themselves, and so again collaboration was the key to making the system work. For people in the core areas of the Ancient Near East, however, the Persians may have represented a passing innovation in that their political and religious centers were all in Iran, and their interests were in the east, not usually the west. Mesopotamians and Egyptians probably thought that this empire too would pass, and they took advantage of what freedoms were afforded by freer trade and travel. In Babylonia, however, where we can trace prices, the Persian period represented a period of inflation, and this may have become a hardship for people living on the edge of starvation. Or perhaps we have a view only of the cities in their scramble for elite imported goods, with agricultural products keeping pace.

A century and a half of relative peace and stability in the Persian empire was disrupted by a young prince from Macedonia in northern Greece who had inherited the loyalty of a group of warrior families from his enterprising father, Philip. This Alexander, later called the Great, followed up his father's efforts to subdue the rest of mainland Greece, and then he turned his attention to the more imposing problem of the Persians. He personally had never forgiven them for the two invasion attempts long ago, and Plutarch (46–120 CE), a Greek who wrote a biography of him, said that he carried with him a copy of the *Iliad*, the Greek poem depicting a late Bronze Age clash between Europe and Asia on the coast of Turkey.

Alexander was personally extraordinary and, from the Persian point of view, completely unexpected. He crashed through the governorships of Turkey, beat a hastily assembled Persian force in the southern Turkish mountains, and pressed on south with his soldiers to take Syria and then Egypt from the Persians. There he paused to consolidate, and he visited a western desert oasis where he became convinced of his own divinity and his greater mission. One aspect of the mission impelled him to found new cities, especially one of several he named after himself on the northwest Nile Delta, Alexandria.

Founding cities was viewed with ambivalence by people in the Ancient Near East, but clearly not in Greece or Phoenicia, where colonies had been thrown across the sea for centuries. If you founded a city, you undermined an older one, the Ancient Near Eastern idea seems to have been, and so it should be undertaken only with great care, as in southern Iraq when the river had meandered away from an old site making it untenable. Alexander had no such fears, and he saw his new cities as focuses for Greek culture as well as retirement settlements for his Greek-speaking veterans and other collaborators.

He pushed on against the Persians and again beat them in the Zagros foothills of Iraq, chasing the Persian king into Iran and into what is now Central Asia and Pakistan. There, on the Indus, his troops stopped him and insisted on turning back. Alexander returned as far as Babylon, where, mysteriously, he died in 323 BCE, only thirty-three years old.

The coming of Alexander did not appear to make much of an impression on most of the Ancient Near East while it was happening, but over time culturally things began to change. Part of that derived from the Greeks' continued desires to rule the area almost as the

Persians had, as the key part of what they later termed the *oikumene*, the inhabited and civilized world. We get our word *ecumenical* from this term, but use it only referring to church politics and efforts to bring together parts of the Christian Church. Alexander's successors meant it much more broadly.

When Alexander died, he had no obvious heir. There was a son, but still an infant, and his generals and their cronies divided up the world that he had conquered. Though they warred sometimes with one another, they all held fast to Alexander's ideas that he and his elite soldiers would make the best rulers of these vast territories. Alexander envisaged integrating Greek ideas with the Ancient Near East and encouraged intermarriage of his veterans with the locals. The dominant party was to be the Greeks, and Greek was used in administration as much as possible, even as they took over old bureaucracies to administer the agricultural lands.

We call this blending process Hellenism, meaning the admixture of Greek institutions and ideas into local cultures, and it seems to have strengthened its influences over time. Negligible in Alexander's lifetime, these tendencies reached farther than his armies had and became a new international style which all rulers in contact with it wanted to imitate.

The dynasties Alexander's generals created varied in power and extent, and for the Ancient Near East the important ones were the Ptolemies in Egypt and the Seleucids in Syria and Iraq. These kings started as allies but were later frequently at odds especially in Syria and Palestine, where their interests clashed. That meant that the Jews, who had not paid much attention to Alexander himself, sometimes got involved in their politics, and the Jewish Maccabean dynasty snatched independence for Israel from 164 to 63 BCE because of Greek dynastic conflicts.

Some aspects of Hellenistic influence seem important in the long run, though others seem trivial. We have already mentioned building new cities as a Greek passion, and a number of new cities sprouted up in the Near East, some of them, like Beroea near Aleppo in Syria, right next to the older establishments but laid out in rectangular blocks with straight streets next to the meandering street patterns of the older cities. These new cities tried to attract trade as well as veterans to settle in them, and the initial competition with the older cities probably everywhere led to an integration of populations. But the Hellenistic street grids still remain discernible in Aleppo's *souk*, the traditional market district.

The cities had theatres, a feature lacking in the Ancient Near East till then, and they may have implied both mass entertainment as well as religious festivals in honor of the Greek gods. This bothered pious Jews, as did gymnasiums. These were workout buildings sometimes with baths where men participated in athletic contests naked. Modest Near Easterners balked. City assemblies, however, probably fit in perfectly with earlier Near Eastern political customs, though the Greek rulers were careful never to give these new councils any real power. More ephemeral perhaps were Greek philosophical teachings, especially Plato's views about a whole world of ideas beyond the unreal physical world.

All these aspects did work their way into Ancient Near Eastern thought and custom, however, and the true toll of this self-conscious Hellenism is not easy to gauge at any one time. As Greek became more prominent, the language replaced Aramaic as the administrative language in many areas, and this may have led to the decline in writing and studying the cuneiform languages too, though it did not displace Aramaic as most people's first language. Greek became the international scholarly language, and many of the scientific advancements discovered in the period can be traced to people writing in Greek whose first language was Aramaic or Coptic. You wrote in Greek because the elites across the whole inhabited world could understand you, rather like Latin in the Middle Ages, or French in the eighteenth century of our era, or English now. The soldiers who came with Alexander probably were not especially literate or devoted to Greek culture, but the cities they settled in were hospitable to later waves of immigrants who were more culturally informed. Relations with the locals who did not speak Greek could be strained, but in the long run these tensions were resolved peacefully, usually through intermarriage. Greeks from back in Greece might find these cities narrow and provincial, but they did tend to sport some of the ornaments of Greek culture, and boys with lots of leisure (*scholē* in Greek, a word from which we get our "school") could learn all about it.

The benefits that had been derived from the Persian united government were mitigated by the Greek states' diversity, and yet the cultural tone may have been the same or nearly the same from the Nile to the Oxus River, now the Amu Darya out in Central Asia. We must remember, though, that some people resisted some aspects of Hellenism, particularly the Jews and to a lesser extent the Persians. These people and the Greeks themselves are the most clearly recognizable descendants of people in the Ancient Near East. This fact may be a result of the limits that Persian and Jewish traditions had set to innovations and, for the Greeks, a result of the force of pride in the innovations. Or maybe the persistence of these peoples' identities has more to do with later vicissitudes they underwent than with their attitudes toward Greek culture.

Everyone in the literate elites made their peace with Hellenism. Sometimes this might mean taking a Greek name that Greek rulers could more easily pronounce, as in southern Iraq. But in another generation local names might reappear, making it seem that the assimilation to Greek taste had been partial and temporary.

The idea of a worldwide empire as first embodied by the Persians was a persistent one down the ages, though rarely achieved for very long. From the west the pesky Romans began to interfere with the Seleucid and Ptolemaic kingdoms and the other Greek successor states until they insinuated themselves into the Ancient Near East, the western part of which became an outpost of the Roman empire after 63 BCE.

Egypt became the breadbasket of Rome itself. The Italian peninsula no longer produced enough food to feed its people, and so transport ships from Egypt were the key to the empire's survival. To the east other forces were at work, and the Parthian kings exploded from Iran to replace the Seleucids in Iran and Iraq. We know little about these rulers since they mostly wrote on perishable materials, but their sculpture continued to show Greek influence, and they clashed with the Romans on the Euphrates for control of the western edge of their empire.

In the 240s CE the Parthians were deposed by a family from Fars province in southeastern Iran who founded the Sassanian dynasty. These kings too clashed with Rome and conquered most of Syria in the early 600s CE. The Romans themselves had split their holdings into a western and an eastern Roman empire, the eastern part centered on Byzantium, modern Istanbul, and the western on Rome. Latin continued along with Greek to be a scholarly language in both parts of the empire, but inevitably in the far West fewer people read Greek, and Latin too died out even as a second language in the East. A major development for the future was that Christianity became the state religion in 313 CE. This was probably a result of long-term mission activity by Christians and their ability to appeal to converts with the simplicity of the Christian story of one God as opposed to the confusion of polytheism. The Eastern and the Western Roman empires diverged in their practices and to an extent in their ideals, if not technically in their understandings of Christianity.

The Sassanians and the Byzantines were both surprised when the Muslims burst out of central Arabia and were able to overtake the edges of their empires, and even to defeat the armies of the Sassanian center. Byzantines retained much of Turkey, only succumbing in 1453 of our era, but the Sassanians were swept away by the new Muslim state. Here again the ideal was a worldwide empire governed from the Arabian city of Medina, ruled by a small elite of people who had known the Prophet of Islam. Religious authority made a difference in this empire in the first generations, but in later times religion may have been seen as a patina applied liberally to the old Ancient Near Eastern imperial ideas. And really religious people dismissed the rulers as irreligious kings, as to a large extent they doubtless were. Conversion was not a goal of the Islamic state, but gradually elites in the conquered areas embraced the new faith and over generations became integral parts of the ruling classes. More gradually other people less directly influenced by cities accepted Islam, although everywhere there were persistent pockets of people who did not, clinging to their varieties of Christianity, usually not the orthodox kind that had been endorsed by the Roman empire, or retaining Zoroastrianism.

THE FADING OF THE ANCIENT NEAR EAST— RURALIZATION OF EVERYDAY LIFE

We are uncertain about when the Ancient Near East ended. Most textbooks are happy to quit when Alexander arrived, arguing truthfully that to study the subsequent world you need Greek language, then Latin, and the Ancient Near Eastern languages did fade from use, first Akkadian, by the first millennium everywhere only a scholarly language, and then, around the 400s, Egyptian hieroglyphics ceased to be written. The Coptic language continued to be most Egyptians' first language for another few hundred years, gradually to be replaced by the Arabic of the Muslim conquerors.

But language use may not really mark important breaks in cultures. Certainly the later history of the Jews argues that new languages may change very little. Jews had their holy language in Hebrew, and many Jewish boys learned some Hebrew to be able to follow the prayers, but dispersion into the Greco-Roman world meant that the home languages of Jews varied with their geography. People in Rome spoke Latin and its later popular forms; people in Alexandria in Egypt spoke Greek and probably Coptic. But the religious attachment did not change with the language change. This aspect of culture probably is true of other groups too, and so the fading of Coptic and of Aramaic cannot in themselves be taken as signs of cultural upheaval.

The persistence of cities has been taken by scholars as a sign that the Ancient Near East may not have ended quickly, though of course the Greeks' newly founded cities had a different look from the earlier ones, as did the cities founded as military camps by the Muslims. Still, the idea of worldwide rule lingered, and the geographical determinants, and the climate, remained similar.

Maybe the long-term break came only gradually as some of the older cities were abandoned because of the meanderings of the Euphrates and the growth of rural life. The population highpoint in southern Iraq seems to have been reached under the Parthians and Sassanians, before the Muslims arrived, and their irrigation efforts were more extensive than those of the Ur III period, an earlier apogee of population and use of the river valley.

Some have seen the coming of the Muslims as bad for irrigation, but now we think they merely inherited a declining population base and saw no reason to maintain complex irrigation systems. What happened, then, is that the city populations gradually drifted away, back into farming and into nomadic herd-raising, now mostly of camels.

This phenomenon can go some ways toward explaining where the so-called third world came from. It was not that the peoples of the Ancient Near East instantly forgot their former glories. Especially in Egypt, where the pyramids gave witness, that was impossible. But some cities became less influential, and some of their functions, as centers for stimulation of innovation, faded.

These statements should not be taken to indicate the entire region became uniformly backward. In Samarkhand in Central Asia especially astronomy flourished, and poets and intellectuals thrived in the courts of small states in northern Iraq and Syria even after the Turkish soldiers took over management of the Islamic caliph, the successor to the Prophet of God, in the 940s CE. The best-selling poet in the United States today was among them, a man called Rumi, meaning "the Roman," who came from southern Turkey, then considered Byzantine Roman territory, and sang of his mystical devotion to God and the unity of mankind.

An important blow to these cities was delivered by the Mongols from Central Asia, who sacked Baghdad, the last Islamic imperial capital, in 1258 CE. They were only stopped in northern Syria by the dynasty that had been formed by freed slave-soldiers from Egypt, or they might have overrun the entire region. This was "the worst thing that had ever happened," according to one contemporaneous observer, but even it did not fully damp the vibrancy of Near Eastern cities.

More devastating for the region was the plague, which hit the cities around 1346 CE and returned frequently. We know that when it got to Italy as much as a third of the population of Italian cities died within days, and Near Eastern cities probably had as bad rates of death. The countryside may have been relatively untouched, and yet the Near East seems not to have recovered from the demographic devastation until perhaps the 1700s CE, when it joined with the rest of Eurasia in an upswing which we are still experiencing. We still do not know its cause.

In the interim much had been lost. Though farmers might recall the names of ancient ruins or memorable kings, it remained for later scholars to unravel the stories to find the fragments of memory preserved.

THE PERSISTENCE OF THE ANCIENT NEAR EAST—THE CITIES AND THE MARKETS

Some of the cities lived on of course, and live on today. Damascus can claim to be the longest inhabited place in the world, and Aleppo in northern Syria has successfully enveloped the Greek city built beside it to such an extent that the grid of the *souk*, or market, can be seen as an essential element in the modern city.

Cairo, founded by Muslim rulers right next to an older Egyptian town, sprawls impossibly across the Nile Delta up to the desert fringes. And it, like many of the others, is still an intellectual center of the first rank and a marketplace where you get the feeling that you could find anything from anywhere in the world, if you knew where to look and whom to ask.

The problems of the cities have been increased within the last thirty years now by the depopulation of the countryside, as thousands of people all across the region have come to the cities in hopes of finding work when their agricultural livelihoods were becoming marginal. Most large Near Eastern cities are now surrounded by makeshift shantytowns where the less successful live, and only in Egypt has the pressure abated for more city services and more decent housing. The Egyptian lack of growth, however, may actually be a bad sign for Egypt as a whole since it does not seem that Egyptians are leaving their cities to go back to farming, but instead they are emigrating out of the country to find more rewarding jobs in the Gulf region's oil economy, and beyond, in Europe and the Americas. Jet travel redistributes the people whom television inspires to seek better lives, but many millions do not have the choice to leave. Population strains and modernization have increased pollution, and car fumes have caused deterioration of the pyramids and other monuments, not just in Egypt.

Near Eastern cities groan under their problems, but their markets are still being used, and not just the traditional *souk*s that are of interest for tourists looking for bargains and willing to haggle for better prices. The last century saw remarkable strides throughout the region in rail and road transportation, and these advances bring not only the hopeful rural poor into the cities but also raw materials that urban entrepreneurs still use to create new products. A further boost to improving economic prospects is the growth of public education in every country; nowhere does this approach in volume and quality what we are used to in Europe and North America, but everywhere schools have been built and teachers hired, and boys and girls too are going to school, sometimes because their use as agricultural workers is not so remunerative as in earlier generations. All governments of the region now have built new schools, trained and hired new teachers, and literacy is advancing in this already fairly literate region. There is no question that over the long run this groundswell of reading and writing (not to mention texting!) will change things profoundly. These younger educated people have the highest unemployment rate of any group, and yet it is hard not to be hopeful that the next generations will see amazing transformations throughout what used to be the Ancient Near East.

5

LITERATURE

By literature of the Ancient Near East we mean texts that were passed down in the stream of tradition; scribes copied them in the course of their scribal training, and so they were texts for use in instruction. Some of them may also have been enjoyed as entertaining. The stories that appeal to us were not the most popular things in the ancient curriculum, or the most useful. Most of the texts we find were lists of omens and other collections that were studied for their practical advantages, texts on astrology, mathematics, and dictionary lists.

Not all texts known from early periods were passed down to later ones. This process has been called the creation of a canon, and it is certainly one that we can catch sight of in the Bible, although there at some early date the Jews returning from Babylonian exile did crystallize the books they had and tried to keep them unchanging. That is not really part of the canonical process in Mesopotamia or Egypt. In those places people recognized that development was inevitable, though, like the Jews, they also venerated old texts just because they were old.

But what is basic? The text we study most these days is the Gilgamesh Epic, perhaps the earliest extended composition that attempts to address culturally significant values that still are important to us today. It is a story about an Early Dynastic king of the southern metropolis of Uruk who may or may not be historical; his name means "Heroic Ancestor," and that is not a name you give to any baby or really anyone still living. He may have lived around 2700 BCE, and if he was not a real person, his story has drawn on the exploits of several memorable heroes who served as models for royal behavior and probably were attractive to more ordinary people too.

We have stories about Gilgamesh only from the Old Babylonian period and after, a thousand years after he may have lived, and they may not have been a unified epic. The epic on eleven tablets was found in the great late Assyrian library and copied around 700 BCE. It is the story of a young king with unlimited powers and unlimited appetites, who was a trial to his people. He even slept with new brides first, with the bridegroom coming second. His people complained to the gods, who created a wild man to be his equal and to try to tame him.

This figure, Enkidu, was a throwback to the way people were before they differentiated themselves from animals. He ran the steppe, the empty area between cities, and freed animals from traps and was in communion with herds of animals. A hunter hired a prostitute to seduce Enkidu; after he enjoyed her for a whole week, he tried to return to the animals, but he was changed, and they no longer accepted him. This may show that human sexuality, involving facing a partner and not just climbing on from behind, was a source of human self-consciousness. The prostitute taught him some of the arts of human living, like eating bread. She then invited him to the city to meet Gilgamesh.

Gilgamesh and Enkidu hated each other on sight and wrestled, but neither won, and when they were both exhausted, they became friends. As the people of Uruk had hoped, the two went on a distant adventure to the Cedar Mountain, far to the west in Lebanon, to kill its guardian monster, and to bring back wood so lacking on the Mesopotamian plain.

When they came home, the goddess Ishtar accosted Gilgamesh, who looked pretty good after his bath, and asked him to marry her, implying he would gain immortality if he did so. But Gilgamesh refused, citing all the former lovers of the goddess whom she eventually abandoned. This refusal may derive from the so-called sacred marriage, where a ruler had sex with a priestess, both representing gods, to ensure fertility. The evidence for this as a habitual practice is slight, but at least one king participated in it. Gilgamesh seemed to be questioning its usefulness, and ironically he also was rejecting a possible path to immortality.

Ishtar was furious and begged her divine father to decimate Uruk by sending down the Bull of Heaven, a destructive monster. But Gilgamesh and Enkidu were strong enough to kill the Bull of Heaven, and Enkidu even threw its thigh at Ishtar, who was screaming in disappointment on the walls of Uruk. She was incensed and demanded the gods kill one of the heroes.

And so Enkidu perished from a wasting disease. Gilgamesh was appalled when Enkidu died; he cradled the body until it putrefied, and then he began to run the steppe as Enkidu had done. He ran, not joyfully and full of animal exuberance, but with excruciating existential sadness. The realization had finally come to him that he too would one day die.

Gilgamesh decided to try to find immortal life. He knew that one human being had attained it. That was the hero of the flood, who had been rewarded for his piety and obedience with eternal life for him and his wife in a distant land across the water.

In a harrowing journey Gilgamesh encountered, in an Old Babylonian version, a female barkeeper who told him his quest was in vain. The best humans could do, she said, was to be kind to those around them and to enjoy their time alive. She seems to give the moral of the whole epic, but later editors did not include her speeches, maybe because they generalized too much.

Gilgamesh did make it to the flood hero, who told the story of how he had obeyed Enki, the wise god of fresh water, who had leaked to him the destructive plans of the other gods. But the flood was not going to happen again, and there would be no other flood hero who might be rewarded with life.

The flood hero and his wife contrived a test for Gilgamesh involving his staying awake for days, but he could not, being really really tired. Finally they told him about a plant that did not offer immortality but only physical renewal, a sort of herbal Botox. Gilgamesh retrieved the plant and, in what may be a sign of maturity, did not immediately consume it; he would bring it back to an old man in Uruk. But even this did not happen since Gilgamesh neglected to safeguard the special plant, and a snake ate it, immediately molting its skin. This is an explanation of the ability of the snake to look younger, but of course human beings could not do that, now that the plant was lost.

Gilgamesh was sad that the plant was gone, but he invited the flood hero's boatman who accompanied him to come to Uruk and observe its magnificent walls. This passage echoed one at the beginning of the epic. The idea was that the building of those walls, benignly protecting human activity, was a worthy monument to human endeavor. The story still attracts us and invites us to consider our own limitations.

There are no epics from ancient Egypt, and yet there is a memorable story that may represent central aspects of Egyptian thought about the nature of human beings. At the beginning of the Twelfth Dynasty in 1994 BCE Amunemhet I again united Egypt, and he devised a plan for succession to the throne; he would make his son co-king, or co-regent, while he was alive.

The Tale of Sinuhe shows it was not a smooth transition. Sinuhe was a court official on campaign against the Libyans with the young co-king when the news of the old king's death reached him. The heir to the throne immediately went back to Egypt to order affairs and oversee his father's burial. But Sinuhe was afraid, probably that there would be a purge of officials including himself, and so he snuck away. This story was frequently copied, and the earliest copy comes from later in the Twelfth Dynasty, the period in which the story is set. It was based on the form of an autobiographical tomb inscription, but there is no evidence Sinuhe existed.

In the story Sinuhe walked from Egypt to the east, across the desert of Sinai and encountered friendly nomads who took him in and even gave him a wife. He rose to become an important man in Syria-Palestine and to own fruitful lands, and he succeeded in beating a challenger in single combat. He was honored among the Syrians and served as an informal Egyptian consul. He had fine sons, but all was not well with him.

Suddenly he got a message from the Egyptian king, forgiving his flight and insisting on his return, leaving within twenty-four hours. Sinuhe joyfully disposed of his goods and land he had in Syria and travelled back to Egypt.

There he was greeted by the king. He was given new clothes, a great house and restored to his former status, but the main thrust of activities on his behalf was preparation of his tomb. The Egyptian assumption was that it would have been horrible for him to die away from Egypt; you couldn't be sure you would make it to the blessed West if you didn't have a tomb in Egypt.

The Middle Kingdom was the time when the fancy grave goods previously limited to royalty and the favorites of kings became more generally available. And Sinuhe's tale may be a sign of that spread of availability. The popularity of the tale probably has to do with its exotic locales, Syria and Palestine being a focus of Egyptian expansion and a place where many readers and copyists had relatives who had traveled, fought, and died.

Another set of texts has attracted the attention of modern scholars, texts inscribed on tombs and later on coffins and papyri, the reed-based paper people wrote on, which recorded spells, magical things to say, which would help the deceased get into the blessed west. There Egyptians imagined life after death would be a lot like life on earth, only forever. These have been called the Pyramid Texts because they were first found on King Unas' tomb in the Old Kingdom, and they developed into the Coffin Texts which were more widespread, and then the Book of the Dead.

The most famous passage in the Book of the Dead is the negative confession where the deceased was told to tell the gods all the things he did not do that were wrong. The Book implies, as much of the earlier material seems to, that there would be a judgment of the dead. This idea was illustrated by the pictures of the weighing of the deceased's heart (see Figure 5.1). What happens if you fail that test? Perhaps you get eaten by a fierce monster sometimes depicted in that scene. But the spell texts assume you will make it; you paid all this money to have the texts copied, didn't you?

We get some insight into the mentality of the Egyptian bureaucrats through their instructional texts, which we call wisdom literature by analogy to the Hebrew Bible's Proverbs, Job, and Ecclesiastes. Scribes were proud to be scribes, but they also emphasized the duty to be careful not to abuse their power. A memorable story of this type is "The Eloquent Peasant," a Middle Kingdom piece that tells the fictional story of a peasant who came in from the west of Egypt to sell some of his farm produce and encountered an arrogant official who confiscated his donkey and his goods. The peasant got an audience with the official's boss and complained that this

Figure 5.1 Weighing of hearts. From the Middle Kingdom in Egypt around 2055 BCE, there were depictions of the testing of the recently deceased person's heart against the feather that represented balance and justice. The kindly jackal-headed god of the cemetery watched to make sure the person qualified for an honored burial. Rendition by A. Day.

injustice was not how things were supposed to go. The official informed the king that he had a very wordy fellow on his hands, and the king ordered him to write down the peasant's speeches. The peasant returned nine times, becoming more and more upset at the injustice done to him, pointing out that the real role of government should be to protect the weak, not to rip them off. In the end the king granted the peasant's petition and punished the official who first took advantage of him.

A Mesopotamian text somewhat like "The Eloquent Peasant" is more ambivalent. "The Dialogue of Pessimism" from first-millennium Mesopotamia is a series of speeches between a bored master and his slave. The master proposed doing something, and the slave enthusiastically endorsed the idea. Then the master changed his mind, and the slave just as enthusiastically endorsed not doing it. This is a humorous sketch of how to be a sycophant, but it ends with the slave saying that the master really would not survive very long without the slave.

How did the ancients think about the origin of the world? The Egyptian "Memphite Theology" was copied in the first millennium but says it was copied from an Old Kingdom text, and that may be true, since it expresses what seem to be some very old ideas. The Theology says that Egypt started by rising from the sea, probably imagining something like the Nile Delta coming out of the Mediterranean. And the main god who effected this transformation was Ptaḥ, meaning "the opener," a god of the Delta. The text says a divine heart and tongue came into existence and began commanding the land to emerge. The god then proceeded to create other gods to administer the new creation. An important part of it was the idea that people who did what the gods wanted would be rewarded while those who did not were punished. And yet human beings were not explicitly created in the text, although all the crafts and skills which the gods loved were fashioned.

A similar Mesopotamian story is "The Creation Epic." This composition may have formed in the 1200s BCE when a king of Babylonia retrieved the statue of Marduk from its exile in Iran. We know that the text was later used as part of the spring new year's festival, where the focus was on the god Marduk, the city god of Babylon.

The Epic focuses on the strife between the great gods and the god of the chaotic sea, Tiamat, whose name just means "sea." This is a sexist poem which depicts Tiamat as deeply evil. She decided to take over the realms of the other gods, and those gods searched for a champion who would defend their temples and privileges. Several of the great gods refused, but Marduk agreed to fight her if the other gods would declare him supreme over them. They agreed, and he armed himself with wonderful spells.

Tiamat meanwhile had elevated a minor god to be her spouse and king of the gods. This god, called Qingu, was not otherwise important.

Marduk attacked Tiamat, who had lots of demons to help her, but Marduk triumphed through the use of his superior spells. This shows that the Mesopotamians thought there was a power of magic that lay above and beyond even the greatest gods, and the proper spells could tap into that power. Marduk ripped open Tiamat, and then he slew Qingu.

Marduk then proceeded not so much to create the world as to organize it, founding cities and temples and setting up the systems under which we live. As a final thought he created humans from the blood of Qingu, perhaps explaining why human beings could be so troublesome to the gods and to each other. The purpose of humans was to serve the gods and make sure that their temples were well supplied and clean. So the image is of human beings as janitors, or perhaps we can say custodians, of the natural world, not with much authority but connected through service to the powers of the universe. This creation vision is not centered on humans; we are useful, but we are peripheral, and we were an afterthought when Marduk had finished everything else.

The text ended with a long exposition of the fifty names of Marduk. These names were tokens of praise for him and his skills, and many of them implied that he had taken over the powers of other gods. These passages edge toward henotheism, the idea that other gods existed but only one was really important.

It is wrong to see any of these texts as authoritative; none would have been accepted as *the* answer about what Mesopotamians or Egyptians thought about creation, for example. In a polytheistic world there was little possibility of having only one view of a question. There might always be another god, another temple, with a different story, in literary texts we do see the range of possibilities. And we can say that some Egyptians and some Mesopotamians valued thinking in these ways to the extent of being willing to devote time to copying and perpetuating these particular words. For that we can be grateful.

6

ART

The physical remains from the Ancient Near East are the things that attract us still, the simple lines of Egyptian chairs, and the dynamism of the tiny gems that Mesopotamians used as personal seals. But as with literature our reactions may not be the same as the views of the ancients. Beauty may be in some sense eternal, but the clichés of what was expected in art were subject to change. We must keep in mind that the artists were always struggling between the accepted forms in their cultures and the possibilities for doing something new.

Royalty early on bought most of the great stuff, and the king's court was always an important market for fine luxury goods. People around the king could set the standard for what was acceptable, and yet they did tolerate experimentation. Two periods come to the fore when we think about innovation leading to change: the Old Akkadian period in Mesopotamia (2334–2190 BCE) and the Amarna period in Egypt (1350–1300 BCE). What happened in each was different, and the sources of the changes derived from different drivers. To understand those changes we need to consider the standards that came before.

In Mesopotamia in the Early Dynastic Period (3000–2334 BCE) the purpose of art was to commemorate rich people's dedication to the gods. Three-dimensional statues show people, probably intended to be particular individuals, in an attitude of prayer, with hands clasped together, to be placed before the statues of the gods.

In Egypt too the earliest material may be connected to royalty. The Narmer Palette (see Figure 6.1) is a slab of inscribed rock that was used as a very fancy make-up dispenser, probably for eye make-up which the Egyptians loved. But its importance does not lie on anyone's face but rather in its attempt to depict the most important event in Egyptian history, the unification of the land, north and south.

The Palette is important also because it is a very early use of the hieroglyphic writing system. The hammer and fish in a box above the picture of the king spell his name: Nar-mer "hammer-fish." The little fellow behind him is carrying his sandals and has his name above him as does the smitten enemy on the right.

Figure 6.1 The Narmer Palette was found at Abydos where Early Dynastic kings were buried upland in Egypt dating from about 3100 BCE and showing the king wearing the crown of Upper Egypt, where he was from, attacking leaders from Lower Egypt's Delta. Rendition by A. Day.

The king was commemorating his victory over the leaders of the swampy delta of northern Egypt. Some swam away through the marshes, but others shown on the reverse were beheaded by the king and his soldiers; the reverse also has loyal soldiers marching above him with their various standards, or flags, showing what counties or regions they were from.

The Palette was propaganda, but most of the art from the Ancient Near East had that function at its beginning. Kings and rich people had these things made to show how great they were. The Palette was a fine example of conspicuous consumption, though at only 25 inches tall (63 by 42 cm) it was not as imposing as some other bigger monuments.

Much later, around 1350 BCE, there is another much smaller thing, a wall relief or slab of stone carved with an image; it is 32.5 cm tall, or about 13 inches, and it was a symbol of somebody pushing the boundaries, maybe both the king and the artists. The Akhenaten family portrait was an ideological statement (see Figure 6.2). The king had changed his name and broken with the worship of the old Egyptian gods. He was devoted to a previously obscure god, the god of the disk of the sun, and in some statements the king argued that there were no other gods except the sun disk along with the king himself; the king was supposed to be the only one who could intercede for humans.

But you see on the relief that the king was fat, or at least paunchy and odd-looking. That may derive from the concentration on the sun disk. The disk shone on all people and revealed their true natures, and the king perhaps really did look odd. Is this naturalism, though, an artistic effort to depict things and people as they were seen? No Egyptian wrote about the artistic approach or talked about naturalism as a goal, and we cannot be sure it really was.

Another startling aspect of the portrait is that the family was there. Earlier kings had sometimes shown a wife, clearly subservient to them, but the whole brood of children was too personal to show. But not for Akhenaten; this is not the only portrait like this, and there are other bits of art emphasizing the intimate paternal love of the king and also the queen for the Martian-looking children. Especially because the king only had daughters, he was trying to establish their connection to him, and to the blessing of the sun disk, in order for them to be in a position to succeed him as king. A son by another mother than the queen did actually become the

Figure 6.2 Akhenaten and family. In the Amarna period, 1350–1300 BCE, the deviant king Akhenaten favored a sort of naturalism and broke precedent by having himself depicted with his family and with his paunch. Rendition by A. Day.

next king, but he might not have been born when the relief was made, or maybe the king and the artist were simplifying a complicated family situation.

Finally we should note the odd way in which the god was shown. He was the disk of the sun, but here he had many hands which reached out in blessing to his divine worshipper, the king, and his family. This device may have been trying to show in almost human form the power of the warmth of the sun, like massaging hands on a hot day.

Such works were symbols of the Amarna reforms of the second half of the 1300s BCE discussed in Chapter 3 above. But that reform did not long outlast the king, and the old religious customs were restored. What about the art? In a lot of ways it too reverted to older, more monumental forms. And yet in some ways the Amarna

Revolution had left a mark on later art. We catch glimpses of naturalism in the depiction of movement, or potential movement, in some artistic pieces. The attention given to queens and children of kings never resulted in explicit family portraits again, but kings sometimes did feel freer to spend time and artistic energy on their relatives. I am thinking particularly of Ramses II's tomb for his many sons.

In Mesopotamia we see a similar playing with clichés. The old way of depicting rulers is best seen in the many statues of the ruler of Lagash, Gudea, from around 2100 BCE, not the earliest stage of Mesopotamian civilization. Gudea was not a king but just a governor of a city serving a distant sovereign. Gudea was shown as rectangular and simple, but highly polished and, when the head was preserved, substantial looking (see Figure 6.3).

Gudea's heads were almost all knocked off in antiquity. Somebody didn't like him. But he wanted to be seen as a successful prince who had rebuilt his city's great temple. He held in his lap the plan for a temple and boasted in the inscription of the care he had lavished on the plan. This is the guy who left the longest composition ever found in Sumerian about how he rebuilt the chief temple of his town.

Gudea sometimes explained the reasons for his having statues carved. He himself was too busy to pray constantly before the god, but his expensive statue could be set up there, and it could be a substitute for himself to demonstrate his constant piety. And so his work had a propaganda and religious motive; he wanted the gods to remember him, as well as his people to notice him and his devotion.

An example for deviation from this artistic norm was actually produced earlier. The Old Akkadian period in the second half of the third millennium BCE politically united the southern Iraqi plain, and late in the period there were several pieces of art that seem naturalistic. Unlike in Amarna Age Egypt we do not see any ideological hint about why this might have been so.

The most striking example was the Naram-Sin Victory Stele. This sculpture in relief was done on stone to commemorate Naram-Sin's victory over mountain peoples in Iran. The stone itself came from there too. The naturalistic aspect of the piece is the muscles of the king and of his soldiers, who were smaller than he was, but carefully carved. The artist did not attack the problem of

Figure 6.3 Gudea was the city governor of Lagash-Girsu around 2100 BCE who had himself depicted here designing the temple he was rebuilding. Rendition by A. Day.

perspective and created various baselines on which to place figures, and there is no doubting that this was a fight in the mountains. The enemy fell back before the glorious Akkadians, and some of the foe shielded their faces from the wonderful brilliance of the king.

The horned helmet the king had on was an indication that he was claiming to be a god since gods wore horns. We talked about his motives for this claim above, but here we get no explanation, just the fact that the king was a god. The inscription says he had beaten the mountain people. The king paid to have himself shown at the pinnacle of the mountain and at the pinnacle of his own power.

The Akkad dynasty ended, but did its influence on art? Certainly Gudea's statue shows that a penchant for clichéd monumental forms was still present, and Gudea was trying to look like a king of his city from before the Old Akkadian dynasty created its empire. But there were flashes of naturalism in later periods.

We see some naturalism in cylinder seals from the Old Babylonian period, around 1800 BCE. Such seals were carved on three-inch or two-centimeter pieces of stone that had holes through them. They are the typical artistic creation of Mesopotamia and were used by people to put their signatures on tablets of wet clay. There was a hole made so the seal could be worn on a cord around the neck. Sometimes seals had writing on them, usually the name and title of the owner. Some have only the design, and in some we might see a fight between the divine king and a writhing serpent-like animal. This may be an illustration of the fight between Marduk, the god of Babylon, and the personification of watery chaos, called Tiamat, "Sea," in the "Creation Epic" discussed above. We know the end of the story, and even if this is not the end of Tiamat, it probably is another rendition of a battle between order and dissolution, chaos and entropy, and here too the forces of order win. The thing to remember about seals is how tiny they are and with what care the artist worked the stone. And though the scenes may be fantastic in that we do not see many real dragons around, the way the thing is rearing up and twisting conveys movement that looks real. Time and energy went into seals, and as in pottery styles and other larger works of art, such things conferred status on their owners, and most were not royal.

We see a last explosion of Mesopotamian natural depiction on the walls of the palaces of Assyrian kings. Here we show a part of a wall relief of the last important Assyrian king, Assurbanipal, 668–627 BCE. He had himself painted (the colors are worn away, but the relief is still there) hunting lions (see Figure 6.4). There really were lions in the hills then, and kings liked to show their prowess against those scary beasts. Assyrian kings wanted to impress visitors to their palaces with their power and wealth, and showing lavish hunting gear and prey was a cheap way of doing that.

The artist of this relief showed the king and his attendant in wooden poses which do not look natural, but they do exude decorum and power. The lions, however, were something else. They were supposed to be fierce, and the artist had studied their muscles and happily drew their details. The point here was to show the worthiness of the king's savage opponent. A slightly subtler point would argue that if the lion could not resist the king, how could a lowly vassal like you hope to do so? So give up now, submit your taxes,

Figure 6.4 Assurbanipal and a lion. The Neo-Assyrian kings liked to have themselves depicted ridding their lands of lions, who were seen as noble beasts worthy of opposing a king. These reliefs were put on palace walls to impress visitors and display naturalism in their depictions of animals. Rendition by A. Day.

and go home in peace. Otherwise the king and his armies will pursue you. And you will end up looking less noble than this dying lion.

In all these pieces we see the thrust of the policy of the rulers. Art was to serve their oppressive desires to keep people in subjugation or at least to make them think that resistance was futile. But also the pieces show the artists pushing in different directions. The king was strong, they show, but the lion was beautiful. The god will beat the dragon, but the dragon whirls alive. And the pride in execution of the artists is obvious, with Gudea's body so beautifully polished, the Narmer Palette so smooth. The kings ruled, but we still see them through the eyes of some of their talented subjects.

LEGACIES

These societies affected later ones sometimes in direct ways and some-times in oblique ways. We cannot always trace exactly how the inter-action might have taken place. But many later peoples attested to their influence, either by asserting, as the Greeks did, that every human institution really started in Egypt, or simply by using the techniques developed in the Ancient Near East to pursue their own agendas. Here we will look at a few areas of endeavor where the influences are clearest.

DOMESTICATION OF PLANTS AND ANIMALS

The innovation of controlling the animals you use and the plants you want to grow was duplicated in the Far East and in the Americas by other hunters and gatherers, but the Near East did it earliest, as far as we can now see. And even if it was not the very earliest, the things that Near Easterners mastered are still the things that most of the world uses for basic production. The grains, the sheep and goats, the cattle, were first tamed in the Near East and spread outwards from there. By 4000 BCE settled village communities spread across Europe, Africa, and Asia.

POTTERY

Connected with this transformation of agricultural life was the inven-tion of pottery. Perhaps it was originally a mistake, some clay container falling into a fire, but people played with this mistake and made pottery a symbol of status and created highly adaptable vessels for all kinds of needs. We find big pots for wine and dainty serving dishes for fruits and vegetables, and lots of specialized beakers for many other uses. Other cultures elsewhere made the same discovery independently, but the Near Eastern innovation along with the slow change of styles allows us to date sites we cannot afford to dig. This legacy of the Ancient Near East is one source of the complexity of our current knowledge.

THE WHEEL

It is possible that this simple but useful innovation was first tried in Central Asia, where it was helpful in devising carts which could carry things more easily than pack animals. But we see it clearly for the first time in the human artistic record in Early Dynastic Mesopotamia. On the standard of Ur, an ornate box with depictions of the Sumerian world at war on one side and at peace on the other, the cart is a four-wheeled affair with wheels made of pieces of wood fashioned together, and it was used in war.

The Mesopotamian river valley might not have been particularly conducive to carts since the big rivers cut across the valley, but wheeled carts supplemented the cheaper river-borne transport and connected the outlying areas to the cities. Perhaps the wheel was only ever invented once since we can watch it make its way into Egypt in the late second millennium, where the most depicted representation of the wheel was in war chariots which had come in from Syria and Palestine. The wheel was absent from the new world civilizations, and its absence impeded their contact with outlying areas. People had to carry produce in by hand or on their heads to their cities, and there was a limit to how far out you could go before the bearers would have eaten up all the produce they carried. The wheel made the old world societies able to spread out more widely, and not just in war.

LITERACY

The problem with the cuneiform and the hieroglyphic systems was not their complexity or difficulty; if they represented your first language, they were easy to learn. The problem was that most families could spare no one to learn them, and the uses to which they were put were on the whole not practical for most people.

Governments needed systems like these for keeping track of surpluses and for commemorating and propagating their public images and for spreading information to bureaucrats. But farmers relied on their oral cultures and local lore for the right times to plant and to water.

Both of the major systems opened out into experiments that proliferated in the second millennium and led to simpler ways of writing. The Egyptian was probably the one that was being imitated by the inscriptions in the Sinai Peninsula and elsewhere, while the cuneiform was the basis for the Ugaritic simplification of the syllabary that gave us the order of our alphabet. How these systems were shared is hard to guess, but they certainly were shared, and we end up in the early first millennium with a twenty-two-sign system that did not represent every significant sound in the West Semitic languages that used it, but enough for native speakers to figure out what was going on. Scholars have called this not an alphabet, but an *abjadiya*, the Arabic word for the system used in that language, which again does not depict every vowel. This simplification may be the most important innovation on the road to the system we are now using. It may not be as nuanced and beautiful as the earlier systems or as the contemporary Chinese logographic system, and yet it is really easy to learn and fairly easy to adapt to most human languages. It has not been adopted everywhere, but it is the source of all alphabetic systems, including the subcontinent of India's Devanagri. The similar system devised by the Koreans owes its origins to Chinese and not to the Near Eastern alphabet, as does the Japanese syllabary. But across the world, even in Indonesia nowadays, many people use the Near Eastern system, as adapted down the ages, first by the Greeks who needed to make explicit the vowels in their dialects.

ACCOUNTING

A logical extension of the need to expand our memories is a system to record our stuff, and accounting may be said to precede the writing systems and to have given birth to them since we have numerical notation tablets throughout the Near East before we have any signs that say what was being counted or to whom it was going. And we must await the Italian Renaissance for the origins of double-entry accounting, where you write down your income on one side of the ledger and your expenditures on the other.

The earliest accounting texts we have just list goods on hand and deliveries, but by the late third millennium in Mesopotamia we do have texts that indicate the goods on hand and then afterwards record the expenditures, ending with the balance to be carried forward. The goods recorded were expensive resins and spices, and the prices were carefully recorded in weights of silver. The goal of these tablets was to keep track of goods and to minimize pilfering. It was not necessary to make economic decisions, and yet it may have served to apprise the people running operations of who was a reliable agent and who was not.

COINAGE

Most of the sweep of Near Eastern history did not need stamps on its silver and precious metals to function in a sophisticated way as a multi-money economy. This means that several different things could serve in the functions of money, as a means of payment, as a unit of accounting, and as a way of storing wealth. Grain was used as the means of payment within large organizations, and precious metals were used for transactions between the large organizations and the outside world.

One way wealth was stored was in silver that had been worked into coils; it was light, shiny, and attractive even for foreign trade since people who could not understand your language still were happy to accept such precious metals in payment. Around 625 BCE in Western Anatolia people began hacking metals off such rings and stamping the pellets produced with symbols and letters from the alphabetic system. Who did this is unknown, and its connection with governments and rights to coin was a later development. The earliest coins were made from electrum, a naturally occurring alloy of silver and gold, and the worth of these things must have been astronomical. And so it is unlikely that they were used to pay anybody but much more likely that they were for storage of wealth.

We begin to see the involvement of states in coinage with the Persian empire and the Athenian silver mines. Athens found it was sitting on mines with tremendous wads of silver, which it turned into coins with its symbols and name on them and exported throughout the Near East.

Arguments have been made, even recently, about how revolutionary coinage was in simplifying commerce. The idea is that having a reliably marked lump of silver frees you up from having to weigh all the time and might facilitate shipments of silver if the coins were accepted on the receiving end too. But it does not appear that the evidence is very good for such ideas. The Ancient Near Eastern economies had been the most dynamic in the world for millennia, and most people probably saw no need for stamps on their precious metals.

SCIENCE

The sexagesimal number system, where sixty was the base number, was devised in southern Iraq and appeared on the early clay numerical notation tablets. This means that though there was a system that changed symbols as you counted up to ten, it reverted to the symbol for one when you got to sixty. Sixty has many more numbers that divide into it evenly than ten has, and this notation system meant that multiplying anything by sixty was simple. The tens-based system derives from the number of fingers and toes we humans have, but in many ways the sixty base is more flexible. It probably reached the cultures to the west of the Ancient Near East through astronomy, where it continues to be used.

The way we measure circles and the way we tell time are base sixty operations, which we have inherited from the Mesopotamians. The so-called Arabic number system derived from ancient India, as did the notation for zero, which the Mesopotamians did without. The use of zero does clarify the meaning of the sign for one when we mean ten or when we mean sixty, but the Mesopotamians just put the bigger numbers first and figured you could work it out for yourself. And so 1 could be one or it could be sixty, but 1, 25 clearly had to be 60+25, or 85.

We have mathematics texts from Mesopotamia from the Early Dynastic and after that only from the Old Babylonian period at the beginning of the second millennium BCE and from the Hellenistic period and later. This hiatus is probably just an accident of archaeology, but it remains to be filled in. There were two types of tablets that scribes copied, tables for use in multiplication and division, and problem texts, which listed story problems one after another. Such texts were used as classroom tools but also as charts to which you could refer. As with their legal traditions, Mesopotamians tended not to generalize, and a single text could contain many repetitions of a problem that was basically the same.

Both of these kinds of tablets were useful to scribes working on archival texts. They needed to see how to multiply and divide, and the problem texts were very practical, sometimes explicitly dealing with real problems scribes might face in assigning the right number of laborers to an excavation project to have it done in time.

The problem texts show familiarity with the so-called Pythagorean Theorem already in the Old Babylonian period, and so centuries before Pythagoras, the Greek sage who conveyed it who died about 460 BCE. The theorem is that the square of the hypotenuse of a right triangle always equals the square of its sides. Babylonians, though, in typical Babylonian style, did not assert that generalization; instead they showed problems to which the theorem offers the solution over and over again. Maybe the teacher elicited a generalization orally, or maybe you just learned the procedure and never uttered the general rule.

The problem texts show a mastery of basic algebra, keeping the halves of an equation equal, though without the Arabic notations that make it easier to grasp. These texts also show that some scribes were not just interested in the practical applications but were concerned about the nature of numbers and how they worked together.

Studying omens was a major preoccupation of the learned scribes, and their efforts to make correlations between political events and other things that happened in the natural world strike us now as misguided. They undertook it with such seriousness and system that it has caused some modern scholars to suggest that the encyclopedic instinct that gave birth to modern science derives from Mesopotamian models. The assumption about omens was that the gods did want to write their wills upon the natural world; you just needed the power of observation and access to what earlier observers had seen to be able to discern the gods' wills.

What you studied could vary, but a favorite and old object of inspection was the livers of sheep. Sheep livers can vary in shape a great deal, and their use at religious sacrifices may have suggested analyzing their bodies for signs. In most periods there were other things the scribe could look at, though sheep livers maintained their prestige because it was expensive to kill a sheep. Most of it got eaten by officiants and bystanders, but the liver could be examined before the barbecue began. Tea leaves and coffee grounds reached the Near East only much later, but the idea was the same as watching the blobs of oil on water to predict the future, and we have texts about that in the Old Babylonian period.

Was this really an empirical effort? Sometimes it looks as though it was, and scholars said they have searched their tablets to find precedents for particular ominous shapes. We used to assume that the models of sheep livers, which we have from the Old Babylonian period and later, were remnants of early empirical observation. Now it seems more likely that they were teaching devices removed from empirical work because even the early ones used clichés to describe the livers. There was a process of logical elaboration going on. A growth or other strange feature found on the left side was a positive omen. Then if the same thing happened on the right side, it would be a negative one.

Such observations over time were compiled into lists that stretched in some cases onto more than a hundred tablets. This mentality of compilation has been called "list science," and it is a basic way Mesopotamian intellectuals approached the world. It proliferated dictionaries which have helped us penetrate the world both of Akkadian speakers and of their Sumerian-speaking predecessors. Even the law traditions can be seen as compilations of just decisions. For us the problem with this encyclopedism is that the omens collected tell us something about what scribes were interested in, but the correlations with sheep livers are for us entirely arbitrary. Unlike the Mesopotamians, we tend to think that the world is an enmeshed mechanism in which many small details do interact to produce change. But sheep livers are only a small part of that mechanism, and their relevance to anything besides sheep is doubtful for us. Mesopotamians on the contrary did not see the world as a machine but rather as a very complex combination of things created and organized by different gods' wills, and omens were a way through that puzzle, a way provided by the gods themselves. Gods were trying to speak to humans, and in these omens they were doing so. What the list science lacked is a clear empiricism.

ASTRONOMY, ASTROLOGY

The study of the stars was practiced as a guide to the changes of the seasons, but this was a practical astronomy which had no predictive ability. In southern Iraq, especially in the period after Alexander, scholars got systematic about recording what they saw with as much precision as their hands, fingers, and eyes could achieve, and they recorded that objects were so many fingers above the horizon on a given night. They observed the movement of the planets, which seemed a problem for them because they did not just wheel around the poles the way other celestial objects did. They were interested too in trying to figure out eclipses of the moon and of the sun. They were not able to predict these, though there were stories about successful predictions, but they could say where the planets would show up when.

Star-watchers compiled texts we call hemerologies, which recorded movements of stars and planets during a particular month, and they also recorded other events that had happened then. This effort led directly into astrology, trying to predict not the movements of heavenly bodies but the affairs of humans on the basis of celestial observations. We no longer have in our colleges and universities departments of astrology because empirically it has been shown that this lore has nothing to teach us and cannot make predictions. This finding does not, of course, keep newspapers and magazines, or the internet, from having lots of daily analyses based on astrology, which readers still find of interest.

For the Mesopotamians as for the later Greeks, there was no boundary between observing the stars and making predictions of human behavior and outcomes. As with other omens, the empirical basis of these predictions is not demonstrable, but it does not seem that later accretions like a zodiac and its signs were devised in Mesopotamia. In the extensive texts that list celestial omens, particular observations in the sky were labeled as foretelling favorable or unfavorable events. Scribes used the same structural logic they used elsewhere, so that what was on the left was good and on the right was bad for the person who made an inquiry. The idea of birth signs and astral influences at birth seems not to have been present.

Observations were meticulously kept, whether or not they could be correlated with human events. Much later the Egyptian astronomer and astrologer Ptolemy wrote that he had star observations from southern Iraq going back from his time in the second century CE to 747 BCE. Recent discoveries among papyri in Greek confirm his claim, for part of the omen collection known in Mesopotamia was translated into Greek. Ptolemy worked to create an ideal model of the solar system, and we do not know whether he got that idea from Iraq; maybe he just got the data.

Both Egyptian mathematics and astronomical observation remained practical in contrast to Mesopotamian, although in the Hellenistic period the regions were joined scientifically and culturally, and so the Mesopotamian advances were shared. In the healing arts the Egyptians were reputed to be very advanced, and yet their conception of how the body worked was as elementary as the Mesopotamians'. In both places, however, there were practitioners who were skilled in plant remedies and in alleviating pain, alongside others who were looking for an ominous prediction of what would happen to people with ailments. The people who predicted outcomes were more honored, but the practical care-givers managed to calm the sick people and to alleviate their pain, sometimes giving them chances to heal. Egyptian medical papyri give more systematic expositions of diseases than anything in Mesopotamia.

THE SCHOOL

In both Mesopotamia and Egypt some people in all periods learned to write and read from their parents, were "home-schooled." But in each river valley and in places in between there were institutions where bright young boys could go to learn the basics of literacy and from there could look forward to productive careers in the bureaucracies. There were some female scribes, but they were probably trained at home or in all-female institutions like the "cloister" of some Old Babylonian cities. Some of these school institutions were attached to temples, and some were run by learned men on their own. We can identify these places sometimes by the accumulation of tablets and papyri that do not seem to be practical archival records but may have been used in teaching to engage pupils. In southern Iraq in the Old Babylonian period there are even texts that were copied by apprentice scribes that describe the routines and problems of schoolboys. In all places it was not the very young who could learn to write, but boys in their late teens with parents who could spare their contribution to labor for a year or two. Everywhere the number of men, and of women when there were some, who could write was very small.

CITY LIFE

Forming larger and larger settlements seems to be a human propensity, but it starts in the Ancient Near East. The cities created many problems for the people living in them, and they were unhealthy places which experience taught country people to avoid. But there were attractions that kept people coming in. Ease of defense was one motive to move to the cities in troubled times. But the possibility of a more stimulating life may have brought in the young and led to the technical and intellectual innovations which the Ancient Near Eastern cities have left us. Nobody among modern scholars has quite captured what was going on, but something attractive continued happening, for millennia. Some of those cities were later abandoned because of rivers meandering away from them, but others are still exciting centers where country folk come to trade, and some to stay. States formed here, and governments concentrated in cities, and the governments became the biggest consumers, as to an extent they still are today.

POLITICAL LEGACIES

Royal authority as an ongoing ideal first appeared in the Ancient Near East. There were problems always in how to convey it to a later generation and maintain legitimacy, a problem our modern dictators still wrestle with. But the image of the king as responsible for all aspects of life in spite of his very limited power to make things happen persists even in the leaders of democratic states. The demands on a king were always unrealistic, and yet they accepted the roles because of the great honor and reputed power that was supposed to accrue to them. We do not hear of likely throneworthy heirs ducking power because of the hassles involved; there may have been some, but they are not the stuff of legend or of history.

Most kings nowadays are ceremonial appendages to nation states, but another more concrete Near Eastern legacy is the idea of empire. Kings did not in general strive for power over other peoples, but enough did and with enough success to have established international hegemony as a policy worthy of pursuit. Near Eastern kings bashed heads to create their empires, but they learned, as perhaps our leaders have too, that international influence only comes through collaborators, local people in the areas to be dominated who find it in their interest to contribute to the imperial effort.

Multiethnic empires are not in fashion these days, though in China we see a relic of one even now. Some would say that since World War II economic imperialism has replaced the more direct kinds of empire that Ancient Near Eastern kings would have appreciated. Economic hegemony may not really be imperialism, but its opponents persist in smearing it with that word, and that itself may be an inheritance from ancient times.

Another Ancient Near Eastern contribution to the practice of government is the idea that you should write down legal cases. The idea was not necessarily to make them enforceable or even to have people appearing in court refer to them. It was rather to set out a norm for behavior that accorded with community values. Morality was not legislated, but it was codified, in the sense of being written down with a view to someone's teaching it in the course of scribal training.

This feature comes to us through the Hebrew Bible, which definitely stands in the Ancient Near Eastern tradition with one important exception. Almost all the law codifications we have from the earlier Near East derived from kings and their clerks, but the Hebrew Bible did not. In fact, the king's role was pretty much ignored, or he was made into a kind of constitutional monarch, when Deuteronomy advised him to study "a copy of this law" to learn to do what was right (Deuteronomy 17:18–19). That absence of kings is significant; it shows the compilers of the Bible did not think these norms derived from human kings but rather from God. Earlier scribes also saw the norms they propagated as being endorsed by the gods, but with the mediation of the king. The Hebrew Bible dispenses with the kings as intermediaries and makes each person responsible for upholding the morality propounded.

Finally in the realm of politics the Ancient Near East was the first to formulate the freedom of the individual as a value to be strived for. This may seem ironic given that rulers were autocratic and liked to portray themselves as powerful. But the old contention that kings exercised Oriental despotism is flawed. The power of kings was limited by distance and complexity, and local councils, certainly not elected but still representative of the elites, actually ran things. They may have valued conformity from those under them. Still, there is evidence that numbers of Mesopotamians skipped out on their assigned jobs, and that for Egyptians the ability to stroll about at leisure was a good thing. Freedom of movement was always possible in Iraq, where the deserts and mountains beckoned. It may have been more controlled in Egypt, and in late periods slaves needed passes to leave their homes. Political freedom may have been harder to claim, but personal freedom of movement was usually possible; kings might want to be Oriental despots, but they usually did not have much of a mechanism for enforcement. And in each of the river valley cultures there were stories about uppity lower-class people who successfully criticized greedy bureaucrats, sometimes with the collusion of the king. These tales reflect a social connection which later kings would love to emphasize; the stories say that the problem was the administrators, and the king himself was concerned with social justice.

ART

The sculptures that have been preserved from the Ancient Near East strike us as odd and foreign, as not really accessible to our aesthetic sense. They did have a legacy among people from Greece and Rome, where aspects of the Ancient Near East were emphasized. Roughly I would classify these aspects as monumentalism and naturalism. By monumentalism I mean the desire among artists to build big things, in Egypt of stone that endures. In Mesopotamia there was the same need for long-lasting witnesses to particular kings, but since stone had to be imported, stone monuments were mostly too expensive. Mud brick could build high, but it also eroded, as in the ziggurats or temple towers. Oddly things that were meant to last in Mesopotamia might be pretty small, like the amazingly long-lived cylinder seals, tiny works of art usually in stone or some other lasting material. These tiny worlds show a lot about the religious ideas and social status of elites, and they are found as foreign trinkets in Greece, Egypt, and beyond. Assyrian relief sculpture on stone can also be seen as a means to perpetuate the deeds of the mighty world-ruling kings, as can the Persian court buildings that remain impressive in Iran.

The other aspect of art arises sporadically and appeals to us more, and that is the attempts of artists to depict things naturally. A lot of Ancient Near Eastern art was stereotypical: a king should look big and strong and be depicted in the bloom of youth. He might be shown larger than other people in his family or his court. But there were efforts by artists to break the stereotypes and play with them. In the late third millennium under the Sargonic kings there are a number of pieces of sculpture that seem to us to be trying to depict the human face and figure and animals as they naturally appeared.

In Egypt in the late second millennium the Amarna Age gives us what may be similar insights into the struggles of artists to show how people really looked, though here too we may be seeing simply a new stereotype. But the naturalism extends from depictions of the king along with his family—a shocking innovation in itself—to efforts to depict not stolid firmness but movement. The dancer raised her foot as if to move to the music of the dance, and the horse looked as if he were straining at the harness. The religious innovations that accompanied these changes were not retained, but down the ages we do see the occasional emergence of naturalistic efforts. The monumentalism was famous, and though never directly imitated, the pyramids set the standard for enormous public art, and later peoples like the Romans and the French just took some of the Egyptian obelisks and set them up at home, even before they could read them.

RELIGIOUS IDEAS

The most influential legacy from the Ancient Near East has been its religious ideas. As we learn more about non-Western traditions, we can more clearly see the contrasts to what the West inherited and in many ways how central these ideas have been to subsequent religious thought.

Most basic is the sense that you only go around once. Though it may be trendy now to think about past lives and reincarnations, the Ancient Near East was having none of that. The human being's life may have been long or short, boring or full of incident, but the assumption was that it was a one-time run. This life therefore mattered tremendously, indeed exclusively; there was nothing else.

Linked to the value of this particular life for humans was the sense of the responsibility of the individual for actions. There may have been times when communal pressures and traditions impinged on what people decided to do, but the trend in the rhetoric of the Ancient Near East was toward the individual taking responsibility for action. The idea of communal responsibility occasionally arose, but it was usually rejected. "Let the sinner bear his crime," the wisdom god Enki advises the high god Enlil in the Gilgamesh Epic. In the first millennium, when many traditions spilled forth reformers who sought to revitalize people's understandings of their pasts, this stress on the individual grew. The prophets in Israel argued it was not enough to be born into the Israelite religion; rote traditionalism was not what God wanted. God wanted individuals to be considerate of the poor. It was a communal obligation, but it was each person's responsibility.

A symbol of this idea of responsibility was the Egyptian vision of the weighing of hearts. This image, repeated on funerary papyri from as early as the Middle Kingdom, showed the dead individual's heart, the seat of reason and judgment in Egyptian thought, being compared to a feather symbolizing *Maat*, the idea of right balance and justice. The dead person was sometimes aided by one of the gods to ensure that the heart was weightier than justice. Ideas about eternal punishment were not stressed in Egypt, and the reward was a continued bliss not unlike upper-class life.

An assumption that may be nearly universal is that the person lives forever. We see this early where grave goods were buried with people. The tombs of Egypt may be the ultimate expression of the continuation of the person in spite of death.

Finally the legacy of most enduring significance from the Ancient Near East was certainly the innovation of monotheism. This idea simplified the roles of humans from the bewildering complexity of polytheism, but polytheism as practiced in the Ancient Near East had many aspects from which monotheism eventually drew. Among these were the gods having distinct personalities and placing moral demands on people. Gods and the one God were assumed to intervene in history and both to impose and to heal evil. Prayer was assumed to be pleasing to the many gods and the only One. The divine will could be inscrutable, but it had to be addressed.

8

THE REDISCOVERY OF THE ANCIENT NEAR EAST

Before the 1720s nobody knew much about any of this because nobody could read the Ancient Near Eastern languages. All except Aramaic had died out as spoken languages, and Aramaic had followed its own course to change and innovate from the language spoken in the first millennium BCE. The written languages lingered longer, but the cuneiform system gave way to the more alphabetic systems and Egyptian just changed its writing from the age-old systems to a new one, based on the Greek alphabet with some additions. We call the result Coptic, referring to the people of Egypt who remained Christian when Islam came.

Cultural traditions did continue, but people were not able to recall exactly what the history of those traditions had been. In place names we still see echoes of the ancient names, and there are many other cultural aspects that continued to be practiced. People were still interested in earlier history, but they were limited to sources that were written in Greek and the Bible, thus emphasizing one strand of tradition about the Ancient Near East but remaining in ignorance about other strands.

What happened after all those years to make decipherment possible was a combination of chance discoveries and new practices, along, as ever, with a bit of luck. The combination of these elements led to what was arguably the most impressive achievement of the eighteenth and nineteenth centuries, the rediscovery of the Ancient Near East.

THE ABBÉ AND THE PALMYRENES

The key ingredient for decipherment was accurate copies of whatever was to be deciphered, and these began to reach Europe in the 1700s with greater frequency. Perhaps this was due to a higher level of art education which European travelers had or perhaps it was a result, a rather distant result, admittedly, of the Renaissance interest in antiquity in general. This is the time of the rise of the antiquary, the person who collected old stuff and tried to understand the culture behind it, especially the local culture. Objects from the East held fascination too, and along with the chinoiseries, the trinkets and cloth from the very far East, came other stuff and sketches of other things that had inscriptions.

The first person to make a contribution to the understanding of one set of relics with writing was the priest Abbé Jean-Jacques Barthélemy, who lived from 1716 to 1795 CE in France. He was steeped in Latin and Greek studies and became an authority on ancient coins, and when copies of inscriptions from the Near East reached him, he began to play with them, particularly the inscriptions from Palmyra, an oasis in the Syrian desert.

He knew from Latin sources that this had been an important trade center until the Romans overran it in 272 CE. He knew some names of rulers and assumed that the Palmyrenes would have been writing in a Semitic language, and his early guesses were based on trying to find words similar to those in Arabic and Hebrew, the most accessible such languages. He divined that the system before him had only twenty-two different signs, and therefore it had to approximate an alphabet, and he began to perceive the meanings of some of the words. The personal names were hard, and they turned out to be mostly Arabic, but the language being depicted was a form of Aramaic, a language known from the Books of Ezra and Daniel in the Bible and the Talmuds.

Barthélemy announced his success in public letters which were printed, and he was in correspondence with most of the people interested in the ancient world in his day. His decipherment was quickly accepted as valid, and he then moved on to tackle the more archaic-looking script from the Mediterranean coast, Phoenician. This was not Aramaic, but it was a language closely related to Biblical Hebrew, and the system of writing was basically the same as the Palmyrene. The contents of both of these sets of inscriptions were formulaic funerary epitaphs and royal propaganda statements, and so not the fine literature that people had been studying from the Romans and the Greeks. But Barthélemy allowed people to read scripts they previously could not, and the long dead began to speak.

The things Barthélemy needed to succeed were the same in subsequent efforts at deciphering ancient writings, but they were not always present in sufficient quantity and quality so as to assure decipherment. The first thing he needed was accurate copies; without those no progress was possible. Sometimes the copies were pencil sketches but sometimes too they were papier-mâché or plaster squeezes from the surfaces of relief inscriptions.

The second thing Barthélemy needed was a guess about the underlying language with which he was working. He assumed that the language would be related to what most of the contemporary peoples around the Palmyrenes were speaking. The West Semitic dialect he assumed turned out to be right.

He also needed a sufficient volume of examples of the signs he was studying to make sure that he could generalize about what each sign was supposed to look like. All of the inscribed objects were made by humans who may not have had a standard form for each sign and consequently had a lot of variation in the signs. This was a simple matter for Palmyrene. There were lots of texts, but they did not say a lot of different things. This feature derived from the formulaic nature of the epitaphs. Palmyrene still does not have very long inscriptions preserved, though other Aramaic documents do have long texts.

A third thing the decipherer needed was patience and willingness to consider small variants in signs; they might in fact not be the same sign, and you don't know if you are coming at a system cold, as Barthélemy was. The Germans call this *Sitzfleisch*, "sitting flesh," the ability to concentrate for long periods on one problem until it is solved.

The final aspect of success for a decipherer was luck. Barthélemy could have guessed that everything was Greek and been completely frustrated by the whole process, but he did not.

CHAMPOLLION AND EGYPT

More famous than Barthélemy is Jean-François Champollion, who lived from 1790 to 1832 in tumultuous France, riven by the revolution, Napoleon, and the restoration of the Bourbon kings. Champollion was an ardent Republican and supported Napoleon—not such a good thing to have done after the restoration in 1815. He studied languages in Paris but ran afoul of the royalists in his teaching job and was exiled back to his home in Grenoble in the southeast of France. He had studied a lot of languages and was especially interested in Coptic, the liturgical language of the Egyptian Christian Church, and had read more in that language than anyone else in Europe in his time.

When he turned to Egyptian hieroglyphics, he found that there was a long European tradition of seeing them as signs that each stood for whole ideas, or logograms, somewhat like the Chinese writing system. We could sometimes see in the picture itself what the meaning was, and yet we could not really read Egyptian.

The Rosetta Stone, so called after the mouth of the Nile it was found near, was a trilingual inscription that said the same thing in three different scripts, and one of them was a straightforward ancient Greek, which scholars could easily read. But there were only about two hundred different words in the Greek and more than four hundred different signs in the Egyptian hieroglyphic section, which was actually only a part of the message because some of the Egyptian section had been broken off.

The second script seemed much more cursive, but again it had too many different signs to be a phonetic system. The Englishman Dr. Thomas Young (1773–1829) gave the Rosetta Stone a try; the British had taken it from the French as they helped them evacuate Egypt, and so Young could study the actual stone. He was able to make sense of the cursive script and to build on the identifications of some of its signs as alphabetic, a proposal that had been made earlier by the Swedish diplomat Johan David Åkerblad (1763–1819). He corrected some of Åkerblad's readings but also showed that there were also word-signs in the cursive system, which we now call Demotic, from the Greek meaning a "popular" form of late Egyptian. In addition to the proper names which Åkerblad had been able to identify, Young had derived a list of Egyptian words from the Demotic text. But he could not read the hieroglyphs.

There were many good copies of hieroglyphic texts, especially as the reports of the scholars who had accompanied Napoleon began to be published, and they were copied by people in touch with Champollion. He had a variety of texts from several periods and was able to construct tables of what the usual signs looked like. Basing himself on the Greek personal names in the Rosetta Stone, he decided to try plugging in alphabetic values to some of the recurring signs, and he derived a list of twenty-four signs that seemed to have a predominantly alphabetic or at least consonantal sense beyond the personal names. But he could not be sure that the practice of spelling out Greek names was really giving him access to how earlier Egyptians wrote. He feared what he had discovered might be because of Greek alphabetic influence.

Champollion tried to use his familiarity with Coptic to work ✗ back to an earlier form of the language as expressed in hieroglyphs. The breakthrough came with two royal names from periods long before there could have been any Greek influence. He saw that a king who built a great deal wrote his name /sun/ /X//s//s/. He posited the /s/ from the transliterations of the Greek names in the Rosetta Stone. And he knew that the Coptic word for sun was *re^c*, where the last sign stood for a sound made by constricting the back of the throat that exists in Arabic. And so he guessed that the ancient king would write his name R^c-X-s-s, and that reminded him of the famous Ramses known to be a builder by the Greek writers. So perhaps that X was /m/. This intuition was confirmed when Champollion was sent a new inscription by a new king which had in first position a picture of an ibis bird, then the same X, and two s's. He knew that the Greeks said the ibis was connected by the Egyptians to the god of wisdom and writing, Thot, and if he put that god's name first, he got Thot-X-s-s, and so Thot-m-s-s was likely. This was the name of another second-millennium BCE king familiar from Greek sources. Further, he knew the Coptic word for "to give birth" was /mes/, and so he correctly assumed that that was the meaning of these names: the god has given him birth.

Champollion in 1822 went into print with his discoveries and began to explain more and more inscriptions with his system. At first there was hesitation among scholars to accept that Egyptian had been cracked and that it was not mainly a word-sign system. But Champollion could read so much and explain even Egyptian grammar to an extent that his decipherment was accepted as correct. In his last remaining decade the young Frenchman got to visit Egypt to study more inscriptions which supported his views. He died of apoplexy in 1832 at the age of forty-one, and in Europe his findings were followed up by many scholars who refined his readings and extended his understandings of how the grammar worked, as well as collecting many more Egyptian inscriptions.

HINCKS IN HIS STUDY

The last great breakthrough into the Ancient Near East was made by Edward Hincks (1792–1866) on the basis of good copies of inscriptions from Iraq and Iran that looked like nail-writing and so were called from the Latin cuneiform. Hincks was born and educated in Ireland when Ireland was an outpost of the British empire, and he earned degrees from Trinity College in Dublin. He was ordained in the Irish Church, meaning the Church of England in Ireland, and spent his life as a parish minister. The key fact about the conditions of his life was that there were not many Irish people who attended the Irish Church since most were Catholics, and so he had a lot of leisure time to investigate his scholarly interests. He personally always hoped for a university position but was disappointed in that quest, perhaps because he was known to be liberal in questions of doctrine. Presumably in Ireland at that time that meant he was inclined to accept non-standard beliefs and perhaps to support full civil rights for Catholics.

Hincks first got interested in the inscriptions at Persepolis in Iran. Georg Grotefend (1775–1853), a high-school teacher in Germany, had figured out that the script was a syllabary and correctly guessed that the language would be Old Persian, an Indo-European language known from much later Zoroastrian religious texts. He had noticed several repetitions of groups of signs and correctly saw that these were names of kings in a dynasty that named children after their grandfathers, as the Persian kings had. This had allowed him to posit several signs as representing a consonant plus a vowel. Hincks was able to confirm this and to extend the number of signs identified and to read off the inscriptions as Old Persian.

After 1846 Hincks got access to Henry Creswicke Rawlinson's (1810–95) copies of the Besitun inscription in Iran which was trilingual. The uppermost inscription was clearly in the Old Persian Hincks had already mastered. The other two scripts were not known, but looked nail-like. Hincks had also paid attention to tablets from Lake Van in Turkey which were also in cuneiform script although used on a language which, we now know, had no connection to the rest of the languages of the Ancient Near East. These texts were formulaic, though, and they allowed Hincks correctly to identify vowels in consonant plus vowel signs.

Being able to read the Old Persian section allowed Hincks to study the personal names in other inscriptions, and he began to work out many of the values of signs which we still recognize. He also guessed correctly that the second Besitun script expressed a Semitic language, which we now call Akkadian. In 1857 the British Academy sent copies of a newly discovered inscription to three experts in the field, including Hincks, and asked them to come up with an independent translation of the new text. When the translations came in, they corresponded to each other in a general way, and the Academy declared Akkadian, then called Assyrian, deciphered. These results derived mostly from Hincks' meticulous efforts.

Most Europeans and Americans were interested in these new discoveries as they might affect what was known from the Bible and Greek sources, but it does not seem that decipherment really changed the way people thought about Egypt and Mesopotamia. The attraction of Egypt had been long-standing for Western popular culture, and the Napoleonic invasion had simply renewed an old fascination. Mesopotamia and Assyria were less well known as paradigms of architecture and dress and so had less of an image to change.

The reception of the new knowledge was affected by diverging methods of publicizing the discoveries. Scientists accompanying Napoleon were encouraged to publish their findings about all sorts of aspects of Egypt, especially by Napoleon's successor in command of the army he left in Egypt, Jean-Baptiste Kléber. But how they published involved years of labor and resulted in a series of huge and beautiful books that were printed between 1809 and 1826 that were far too expensive for normal people to afford. Libraries and institutions got these books, but what was in them remained accessible mostly to scholars. Cheap editions featuring the drawings are now available, but they were not in the nineteenth century.

The British meanwhile had found amazing things in Iraq, and Austen Henry Layard (1817–94), the first excavator, rushed to print with cheap editions of his books which sold well. When the British Museum began displaying some of his finds, crowds thronged the exhibition perhaps because they had seen the prints in Layard's books and read the descriptions. And so there was in the English-speaking world a more widespread fascination with the ancient discoveries than on the continent, at least initially.

THE ANCIENT WORLD EXPOSED—FROM FLOOD STORY TO BIBLE AND BABEL

The ancient art allured, but it was the texts that proved to be the bombshell that made ancient history part of the cultural conflict of the late nineteenth century. The masses of archival texts and the royal inscriptions did not excite too many people, but the literary productions did find readers. A British Museum drudge named George Smith (1840–76) taught himself to read cuneiform, and he came across a story that he recognized as the narrative of a primordial flood in which most but not all of mankind had been destroyed. This tale was part of the Epic of Gilgamesh, known from tablets copied around 700 BCE, though we now know there were similar stories in Iraq a thousand years before. When Smith published his understanding of the text, a London newspaper offered him money to go to Iraq and find more of the story. Amazingly on his first day on the mound of Nineveh in northern Iraq he did stumble upon more of the tablet.

The flood story posed the question of what the relation might have been between the well-known Biblical stories and the Babylonian background. Perhaps the Hebrews were just reworking old tales with their one God replacing the many gods of the Mesopotamian stories. But if so, what other changes were made, by whom, and when? These questions are still open ones, and at the time there were some scholars who went so far as to say that the cuneiform material was older than the Bible and therefore better. This argument, made most famously by the leading Assyriologist of Germany, Friedrich Delitzsch (1850–1922), may have had an anti-Semitic tinge to it, rejecting what Jews had created in the form of the Old Testament in favor of earlier stories produced by other Semitic speakers, which Jews had copied.

Delitzsch called his lectures on the subject "Bible and Babel." They offended the German Kaiser, before whom the first one was read, but they were translated and studied by students open to critical study of the Bible. Others felt they had to reject the new knowledge as inherently blasphemous if it undermined the Bible. More moderate voices noticed the continuities with the Bible but also the divergences and saw in the Biblical stories ones related to Mesopotamian and, to a lesser extent, Egyptian precedents, but with considerable creative updating.

Connected to this debate was the issue of chronology. The Biblical chronology suggested that the earth was about 6,000 years old, meaning that it had been created in 4000 BCE. It was not clear at the time how much older the oldest texts found were than the Bible and the Assyrian period, but it did seem that textual material went back perhaps two thousand years before that, leaving not too many years back to creation itself.

The new science of geology too challenged Biblical chronology, and a number of people found the whole issue disturbing. If the Bible was wrong about the date of creation, what else might it be wrong about? Generations of Biblical scholars have gradually integrated the new knowledge of the rest of the ancient world into the understanding of Biblical texts, and yet still the challenge to a simple Biblical faith may be bothersome to some.

The discovery in 1901 of the so-called Code of Hammurapi (then: Hammurabi) was also disturbing because it had close parallels to the laws in the Bible about debt slaves and the very same goring ox problem. Did Moses read cuneiform, people wondered? We still do not know how these cross-fertilizations occurred, but most scholars now accept that though Moses probably had no direct access to Hammurapi, he or whoever wrote the legal sections was exposed to Ancient Near Eastern legal ideas. And Hebrew law may be seen to an extent as a reaction and criticism of some of them.

People committed to the Abrahamic faiths want to emphasize the uniqueness of the Israelite contribution to human thought. There can be no dispute, however, that the Israelites made their contributions in the context of Ancient Near Eastern ideas.

THE ANCIENT WORLD USED—BIBLICAL ARCHAEOLOGY

Archaeology has become more systematic and scientific since the nineteenth century, and the effort has been focused not just on recovering great buildings and great art but also houses of ordinary people. Archaeologists try to understand the economic bases of ancient prosperity and decline. One aspect of that systematic effort was the development of pottery chronologies for many areas, and these charts of changing pottery styles allowed scholars to date sites in relation to other sites as soon as they had an idea of what pottery was used when the place was occupied.

William F. Albright (1891–1971), an American scholar, was the innovator in this effort in Palestine and Israel. He and his students were motivated, as many nineteenth- and twentieth-century scholars were, to try to see if the Biblical tradition could be meshed with archaeological data. This effort achieved remarkable breakthroughs in the understanding of the group of texts called the Dead Sea Scrolls, which give the earliest extant manuscripts of parts of the Bible, some from as early as 200 BCE.

And yet in other areas, Biblical archaeology faced undeniable problems. The conquest narratives in Joshua and Judges in particular were not on the whole supported by archaeological excavations. Jericho was empty in the period when the Israelites were supposed to have attacked it. And the early kings of Israel were not found in inscriptions, either their own or of their contemporaries, except eventually for a vague and broken reference to "the house of David."

Albright and his students remained convinced that the Bible was mostly right about historical events, but there have arisen critics who have been much more skeptical about what can have been known to the people writing the Bible hundreds of years after events. Most will admit that some historical memories persisted, but details would probably be updated, as when a Genesis narrator says that Abram came from Ur and adds "of the Chaldees" (Genesis 11:27–28). There were a few towns called Ur, and he wanted to make sure you knew it was the southern Mesopotamian one, but the Chaldeans had only been around since the middle of the first millennium BCE, and Abram was supposed to be living more than a thousand years earlier. This text was updated, and others may have been too. But if so, the kind of information that might be confirmed by archaeology and close readings of Mesopotamian and Egyptian texts would not be likely to be forthcoming.

Still there are people trekking off into the Turkish mountains each summer looking for Noah's ark and other artifacts. The way most people get interested in the Ancient Near East continues to be through their reading of the Bible, the classical texts, and in the Arabic-speaking world through interest in the prehistory of Islam. The curiosity about the earlier world continues, but it seems that the Ancient Near East as a whole is destined to be seen by most people as a precursor to our contemporary religions and not as an area of inquiry in its own right.

CONCEPTUAL AUTONOMY

This was the feeling that inspired the German scholar Benno Landsberger to write a 1926 essay in which he argued that the cuneiform world especially should be seen in its own context. A Jewish scholar who would face years of exile because of Hitler, first in Turkey and then in the United States, Landsberger was calling especially for the material studied by Assyriologists to be separated from Biblical subjects but also from Arabic studies too. He published his essay in the journal *Islamica*, which focused on Islamic religion and Arabic.

Landsberger wanted to show that speculations about the origins of Hebrew words frequently had nothing at all to do with the use of similar words in Akkadian. Not only was there a distance in space and time, but the Mesopotamian language retained deep influences from early interaction with the unrelated language of the Sumerians.

Landsberger's call for independence has been answered in various ways, and in some other ways it still continues to be resisted. He was working in the period in which all scholars had to compile their own dictionaries, and you were forced to rely on etymologies from other Semitic languages. Increasingly after World War II the great dictionary projects in Germany and the United States, the latter under Landsberger's own leadership, could be consulted. What these books showed was just the conceptual autonomy, or independent ideas, that Landsberger had called for. Mesopotamians were in a world of their own which had to be understood in its own terms, which, the dictionaries demonstrated, were legion.

Graduate training has followed this insight, and students have become more specialized earlier, usually concentrating in their study on texts from one period of Mesopotamian history. Egyptologists have remained more interested in the history of art, but in Egyptology too there has been an increase in specialization. This trend has to do with the professionalization of the academy in general, though, and also with the way our knowledge of the Ancient Near East has developed.

The unfortunate aspect of this specialization, an aspect shared in many other fields of inquiry, is that students have trouble addressing broad audiences about their findings, and the field of popularization has been too often left to journalists and others with no immediate knowledge of the texts, art, or architecture involved. But we should be happy that people are interested still, and that when people ask questions about origins of techniques and institutions, there are answers available which were not there before the Abbé Barthélemy tackled Palmyrene.

HISTORY AS IMPERIALISM

Or was the entire effort to understand the Ancient Near East just an offshoot of British and French imperialism? As mentioned in Chapter 1, this is the argument of the late Edward Said's 1978 book *Orientalism*, and in the era of decolonization and the condemnation of imperialism the argument has had wide, if too uncritical, circulation. Said (1935–2003) felt that in the Muslim world especially the people who came to study the languages of the region tended to be imperial administrators, like Henry Creswicke Rawlinson (a diplomat, however, not really an imperial administrator in Iraq, though he had been that in India). Their command of the modern languages was helpful in manipulating the natives. But Said makes the grander claim that the emphasis of early Orientalists on trying to recover early stages of languages was intellectually imperialistic. The scholars were tacitly saying that the contemporaneous people were epigones, unworthy successors of great classical civilizations, and they were too ignorant even to know what they had lost.

People in the Middle East now who are exposed to their ancient history through schoolwork and visits to archaeological museums and sites can understand the attraction. And the Ancient Near East has been explicitly used by modern nations to emphasize their continuities with the famous peoples of the distant past. In Egypt we see that in the nineteenth century already the popular press understood the value of studying the ancient past. Though there were few Egyptians who tried to learn hieroglyphics in the early decades, eventually there were several, and a native school of Egyptology was founded. This was under the tutelage of the foreigners who came to study, and, until the Revolution of 1952, even the head of the Department of Antiquities continued to be a foreigner.

The reaction to Said's book was negative among those studying the Ancient Near East, and his characterization of the field was felt to be skewed and unfair to the many intrepid people from Europe and America who went to the Near East when it was not easy to do so with no view to dominating it politically in any way. Many worked long years in difficult conditions, and when they reflected on why, most said it was for the greater glory of the whole human race and the exaltation of the peoples of the region. Many Westerners found the Middle East backward culturally, but ancient history was an eloquent argument that it had not always been so, and might not be so again. In contrast to other developing regions, the Middle East before oil was a leader in learning and literacy, but it was different from Europe and America.

As we noted above in Chapter 1, Said in later years admitted that he had been too harsh on the Orientalists. And when it was pointed out that both in Egyptology and Assyriology a leading role in the last two centuries was taken by German speakers, who did not ever have any direct imperial involvement in the region, though in World Wars I and II they certainly would have liked to, he admitted that he had not been trying to portray the whole field. Late in life when I spoke with him, he admitted that was an important omission which derived from his bad German.

The basic question is whether Western interpreters have allowed the modern peoples of the Middle East to speak for themselves and to cultivate voices that have been listened to by opinion makers in the West. Have the Orientalists been drowning out what they have to say, partly on the basis that the really important periods of intellectual development in the region were in ancient times? This question is worth posing, and yet it seems to me there is nothing intrinsic in the study of ancient matters that denies the importance of contemporary thought. Indeed, it may give that thought depth, and at least old stories on which to reflect. It may be true that few Westerners read books first written in Arabic, except those who have to for their work. That may be to an extent because of censorship within regimes in the area, though that may be becoming less of a problem in the wake of the 2011 Arab Spring of reforms. The awarding of the Nobel Prize for Literature to the Egyptian novelist Naguib Mahfouz in 1988 marked a watershed; now people do read his books, at least, in translation. Other voices have definitely followed his success.

In the countries of the region besides Egypt there are fledgling groups of scholars struggling to research and teach ancient history and its languages, and, as in the West, their intellectual position is marginal. Unlike hard scientists and even practical sociologists, what they contribute to their students is hard to measure, and jobs in the field are few. But the study of the human past does in fact humanize, and their efforts, exactly like ours, must be chalked up, in the terms of one of Eudora Welty's (1909–2001) short novels, as *Losing Battles* (1970). The students never completely understand, and so many drop out, and that can be disconcerting. Still, it is important to continue fighting for the right to teach and to expose new generations to the depth of our common history.

Those of us from the West must always be sensitive to slights we may be inflicting on people from the region. But we must also stand ready to help in their scholarly advancement whenever possible. That is not because Said has made us feel guilty about the past but because nations who understand and value their own pasts preserve it for future thought and analysis.

HISTORY AS RECONCILIATION

There are many stories about how modern peoples of the region have competed to adopt ancient achievements as their own and to emphasize those of their distant ancestors over the achievements of their neighbors' ancestors. It is natural that people should be proud of what is found locally.

We can see some of that in the efforts of the Middle Eastern and other states to recover parts of their ancient heritages that had been shipped off to European museums before those states were constituted. These efforts inevitably arouse conflicting feelings in Westerners. On the one hand it is convenient to be able to look at antiquities in commodious surroundings in Western countries with relatively rational curators and curatorial rules. On the other, though access may be in various ways more difficult, should not the lands of origin be able to study close up the magnificent aspects of their heritage?

And the questions about studying or not studying items that were looted during unrest in Iraq after the two Gulf Wars and smuggled to the West are not easily resolved. Some scholars do not want to lose the chance to study hitherto unknown tablets. Others worry that studying the texts and artifacts makes them more valuable to the collectors who have bought them, and this in turn may encourage more looting because sometimes desperately poor locals may want to trade these incompletely understood objects from the distant past for easily understandable money. But doing so disrupts the archaeological context in which the objects spent the last millennia and renders them less valuable to archaeology and to history. We can never know for sure what sites looted objects really came from or what their organization might have looked like when they were left by their ancient creators. When we do find objects where they were left, we can understand much more about their uses and roles in that distant past. For looted items, such aspects will forever remain unknown.

People concerned with the ancient and not so ancient past ought to avoid buying antiquities of any sort in order to tamp down the market in them, and we should encourage modern people living near ancient sites to leave them be until later generations of more sophisticated archaeologists have a chance to study them. This is true not just of old world artifacts but also of Native American ones. These too have contexts which are lost because of pot-diggers.

Another productive way to encourage reconciliation between peoples over the products of the ancient past is to attend exhibitions. Usually this directly benefits the states that lend artifacts, and the crafts frequently for sale at such shows directly benefit modern craftspeople. These shows demonstrate the eternal fascination with old things and the continuing wonder people have before the very ancient. We ask ourselves what it was like to sleep on a pillow that was a post with a stone headrest, and we reexamine our own feelings about death and the afterlife. These are humanistic impulses that should be encouraged, but still we can understand ambivalent feelings when poor peoples of the Middle East cannot afford to come to see such magnificent things even in their own lands.

Westerners reading about and studying the ancient past give value to the achievements not just of the past peoples but also their descendants. It is easier to find books in libraries about ancient Egypt than about modern Egypt, and that probably should be taken as a gauge not of lack of interest in the modern region but of the deep allure ancient magnificence still has. Part of that allure may be that the stories may be simpler and less freighted with modern problems. Westerners, like people in the region, sometimes just need to escape into imagined worlds, cloud-cuckoo-lands of the imagination, informed by ancient artifacts and stories, sometimes posing interesting questions of what might have been had things turned out differently, but mostly not involving oil politics or poverty. Some ancient historians may find this process unenlightened, but I welcome any interest at all. For ours will always remain an esoteric area of endeavor which will attract few serious students in any generation. There is no money in it, and jobs are few. But you can read stuff nobody has looked at for three thousand years. The study itself is the reward, and the more people who are made aware of it, even in trivial ways, the better.

In post-apartheid South Africa and elsewhere there have successfully been established panels for reconciliation. These groups research the past and the injustices done and attempt to bring together surviving perpetrators and surviving victims. The goal is usually not judicial, and punishment is not envisioned; the really bad stuff has already been dealt with by the courts. But judicial decisions do not effect real reconciliation. Instead what is needed is serious consideration of the bad things in the past with a view to establishing or reestablishing the human dignity of both parties.

Nations have not always been eager for such inquiries; sometimes it is more comfortable to believe the useful myths of the past. And yet France and Germany both have confronted the atrocities in their histories. Raw wounds will continue to be exposed by the study of the past, but the distantness of what happened in the Ancient Near East can seem to alleviate the injustices.

This is nonetheless the arena in which Jews and Arabs clash about claims to the lands of Israel and Palestine. Outside observers can easily envision compromises that would be beneficial to both peoples, but the injustices of colonial powers on the Arab side and the injustices of Nazism on the Jewish side continue to make the area full of strife. Recourse to ancient history as a charter for rights to the land is still attractive. "We were with Moses," one side says. The other responds, "We are still the Amelekites and the Canaanites and we were here first."

The nationalist identities now defended are relatively recent. Jewish nationalism became a force only toward the end of the nineteenth century, and Arab nationalism in World War I and its aftermath. Recentness does not deprive national aspirations of legitimacy, but it does underline how ancient stories have been used to argue issues which would have been completely unfamiliar to ancient peoples. These disputes raise the question of whether any consideration of ancient history has an influence on modern nationalist debates; certainly there is a potential for contributing to divisiveness.

There is also a potential for more concrete reconciliation. People from very different religious and ethnic backgrounds do work on ancient issues without trying to contribute to modern debates. As more of that collaboration becomes possible, through a softening of borders and of attitudes by way of the internet, perhaps we will see new collaborations that will tend to underline our shared human heritage.

When I was a Fulbright researcher at the University of Aleppo, I helped my Syrian students get books, so the students could write their Masters theses. One evening when I had handed over one of those invaluable tomes to a student, he thanked me and surprisingly said, "You know, there is a great library on ancient history in the region." I was shocked. "Where?" I asked. "At the Hebrew University in Jerusalem," he replied. "It is sad that we cannot go there now because we are at war with the Israelis." "Maybe later that will be possible," I lamely said. He replied, as so frequently you do in conversations in Arabic, "*Inshallah*, If God wills … "

9

LIMITS OF THE FUTURE

At the end of this quick tour of an ancient world it behooves us to consider the broader context of our understanding of the Ancient Near East. Two areas are worth discussing at this point. The first is how we know what we know through language study, and the other is the likely state of historical study in the foreseeable future.

PHILOLOGY AS QUEEN OF THE SCIENCES

Philologists, people who poke at languages, are always grasping only a small part of the intended meanings and probably mostly missing the nuances, doing a less good job at interpreting than the most rudimentarily experienced dragoman from the time itself. We are always clumsily piecing things together that were perfectly obvious to native speakers, when there were native speakers.

This is what we mean by philology, and we need to address the issue of how philology understands things. The study of ancient texts reveals undreamed-of riches, at least in the simple depth of history and of human thought. It would be a crime to omit these subjects from any undergraduate's education—though I am well aware this crime does occur quite frequently, at least in North American universities. Are we impossibly arrogant when we come to study these texts, or is this perhaps really the only kind of knowledge there is? By this I mean that the human mind is structured so that a great deal of our knowledge is in the form of language. We recall images, we recall smells, but we speak of them, we write of them.

It is possible that the study of the brain will one day allow us to disentangle how all of this works, how verbalization facilitates understanding and analysis. We can see it every day all around us. Students who write about a subject know it better than those who simply hear about it. Students who actively try to teach a subject remember more still.

In the human sciences there has been for the last thirty or so years a so-called linguistic turn, where students have maintained that everything is a text and all we have is our own personal perception of language when we try to understand the world. I am not saying that exactly since I, along with practically all working historians, actually think the observed world does exist apart from my perception of it. But it is also my conviction that we mostly react and interact with it through speech. This means that knowing how to understand speech, especially speech formally preserved in some sort of writing system, is among the most important things we can do.

This is not simple. It is as hard as understanding what other people we are physically present with say and intend to say, reading their rhetoric but also their implications through body language. Human beings, even live ones we can talk to and question, are notoriously indeterminate, unclear and full of under-lying assumptions and unspoken feelings. We can ask our living fellows what they mean, but we may not get a straight answer, or any answer.

A text from someone dead is harder. We can only get at the assumptions of the dead people by looking at lots of texts, preferably from the same person, but frequently in the ancient material only from somewhat similar persons. We are thus immersed in a sea of clichés, though we may not be able to see them as clichés or understand what they mean to imply. This may mean that all of our readings of such texts are flat and pedantic, not displaying the wide range of meanings and humor which living people reveal daily. We level off the old poets and make them clear to us. We steal their oddness and put it into our own dear, uncreative tongue. Unless we are ourselves poets, we may not be able to imitate even at a distance the brilliance of the original. "To translate is to traduce," the Italians say, but we do it anyway because we want to know what the ancients said, if only, inevitably, approximately.

All language is full of clichés; otherwise we could not understand it. The words I just used have been used many times before, and anyone who reads English will be able to decipher them. And yet these particular sentences have never before been written. In fact I have never seen anyone in the ancient fields reflect on these problems. Nonetheless I cannot think that my worrying about them is entirely original since they seem to be at the very heart of the discipline of reading and trying to render into modern languages the thought of the ancients.

We start in philology with the system of writing. If it is the same as that of our native language, we may be ahead of the game, or we may be kidding ourselves into thinking we understand how it worked in the past. Everything about how the ancient one is used has to be learned from examples.

Once we have a certainly fluency with the writing system, perhaps we can understand some of the words the dead left. We can do that by comparison with other texts read earlier and ensconced in the dictionaries compiled in the last century. These meticulous compilations build a web of clichés which we can mine especially if we keep in mind the great freedom scribes had to spell the words they wanted to express.

What we know from these dictionaries comes from the texts that were studied and catalogued in the 1920s and 1930s and the judgment of scholars then about what was important in the histories of the languages studied. They tried to explain the words that were found in the texts that were popular within the ancient cultures and also the ones that appealed to them. These were not necessarily the same thing. The scholars of the 1920s and 1930s were interested in canonical, or literary, texts, and they were interested in legal texts. They were much less engaged by archival or economic texts. Like the statues of the Old Kingdom Egyptian kings and the occasional depiction of Mesopotamian monarchs, personal quirks were not stressed but instead the exemplary characteristics, and the wisdom that made kings and courtiers great, not the jokes that made them memorable to their contemporaries.

And so the ancients emerge as flat and pompous, stupidly concerned about precedence and achievements that have in the interim faded in importance. Flat and pompous as the ancients may seem, when we read their texts we may not look up the clichés because for the most part we are familiar with them. But many terms remain only loosely defined; we know they refer to plants or diseases, but which exactly are guesses.

Such guesses can be based on analogy to terms in other languages, and this has been usually helpful when there are languages extant that have been shown to be genetically related to the ancient tongues. This kind of comparative effort was earlier very important in establishing general meanings, but these days it is less used because we seek more precision from the contexts of the ancient languages we wish to understand. Also there has definitely been a reaction to the idea, current at the beginning of the last century, that all the Semitic languages were closely connected in culture and history too, not just in vocabulary. This sort of historical linguistics is the basis of all we know, and yet its limits are clear.

Ancient Egyptian is in some ways even less well understood in its grammar than the Mesopotamian languages because its writing system did not depict vowels, which did make large differences in meanings. For native speakers the ambivalent script was not so ambivalent since they knew what clichés to expect. But we often do not.

We see as through a glass darkly, and there is virtually no possibility this situation will get markedly better. And yet we persist in our imperfect understandings. The reason for that may be found in a literal translation of the word philology. It means "word love." I take this to mean the love of the sound, meaning, and combinations of human expression, starting with the individual word and building up to sentences and to longer compositions and to cultural ideas and even to cultures themselves. The love is the *philia* kind, that is, brotherly love, not sexual or spiritual, but it is nonetheless love.

Philology as an academic discipline is no longer separately professed in the English-speaking academic world, though it persists in German-speaking areas. What it meant in the 1800s was the careful study especially of ancient languages and the texts conveyed in them with a view sometimes to generalization about the progress or lack thereof of human cultures. Its origins probably were rooted in the idea that modern students might be able to reconstruct aspects of the past better than the ancients themselves had been able to do. In part this was felt to be so because we moderns were apt to be more critical about the sources of information and perhaps not so gullible about what might be unlikely to have happened. The scholars who made such proud assertions were influenced by trends in their own cultures and were not able to obtain an unbiased view of events they were trying to describe. But they did present plausible worlds which their contemporaries found accessible and stimulating.

Criticism is at the heart of this word-love, but criticism does not mean carping or rejecting accepted opinions just for the fun of it. Criticism means making distinctions, and the distinctions to be made are among possible suggested reconstructions, of words, sentences, compositions, and events. And the basis for criticism is human reason, not the preponderance of tradition.

You can see why this might have posed a problem for the authority of the Catholic Church and other organizations which relied for legitimacy on the weight of tradition. To allow even learned individuals to use their reason to tease out the most likely scenarios in the past would free them from some, though not all, preconceived ideas, and might lead almost anywhere.

Philology is definitely an Enlightenment idea. The Enlightenment was a vaguely defined period from about 1750 to 1815 or so in which Europeans and Americans too sought to use their understanding of reason to solve problems, not necessarily with attention to what was the received tradition. The political results of this effort could be explosive, as in the American and French Revolutions. But gradually most Euro-Americans came to feel that human institutions were man-made and could be altered by people. Some wished to believe that God had ordained some of them, and others merely felt old things should be retained because they had worked for so long. The radical nature of the Enlightenment made it seem dangerous to lots of people.

Philology was supposed to be the exercise of reason on the remains of human cultures, and its methods lasted into the periods after the Enlightenment, when Romanticism seemed more important. Romantics felt that reason should be replaced by feeling. And yet Romanticism also had the idea that words and languages embodied something special about the people who spoke them.

People expressed themselves and their individuality, but they also tapped into some wellspring of the language itself, which might be equated with the culture, Romantics believed. And so philology became if possible even more important than it had been. Romantics asserted that we need to study not just the ancients in a way to get at their essential spirit but even our own contemporaries who were steeped in oral culture, for there we might find the spirit of our own folk and learn valuable lessons about our own uniqueness and those of our ancestors who spoke the same or similar languages.

In the English-speaking world, though, the term faded, and the task was divided among departments dubbed "Classics," and others devoted to "Modern Languages," and the slack from the hitherto unstudied non-European world was taken up by what became "Anthropology" and "Linguistics." But still at root the Euro-American academies were proliferating texts that needed to be read and understood, and in interpreting these things and to an extent the cultures behind them, philology continued to be queen of the sciences, that essential skill without which actual understanding cannot be acquired.

HISTORY TODAY

I take my title here from the wonderful British history magazine with great pictures and articles written by distinguished scholars. The emphasis in it is frequently Britain and Europe and their former colonies, and sometimes the ancient worlds, meaning Greece and Rome, are featured. I have seen little about the periods we have surveyed here. But I am not complaining; I should be writing such stuff myself, and choosing great pictures.

History has two definitions in English. History is stuff that happened in the past, which stays pretty much the same, as far as we can imagine. The other meaning is the explanation a culture gives of what happened in the past, meaning in our case the discipline of historical study. The sentence before this reflects approximately the definition of history given by the distinguished Dutch medievalist Johan Huizinga (1872–1945); he meant to stress that non-Western cultures might not be writing books that correspond exactly to Western history books, but they definitely are rendering some account of their pasts. It might be in poems, in oral literature, in art, but it has a purpose of preserving memories. It strives to remind people of things in the past.

The reasons people might want to do that can be of several types. They may wish to build on a shared identity, or to create a new one, as in the case of nations recently formed. The Iraqis after 1920 created textbooks that retold the stories of the forty heroes who came from Iraq and made a difference in world history, and they included Sargon, Hammurapi, and Nebuchadnezzar. This sort of history, which is still important everywhere, serves to cement nations and their institutions and to build solidarity of a sort.

Other motives include a quest for origins of our own institutions or techniques, and this quest can lead you far beyond your own time, place, and identity. There may be some continuities with other people, but there will also be major differences. This may not be a quest for identity at all, but just a curiosity about beginnings. The problem with seeking origins, even when they are actually accessible, is that they do not necessarily help explain later uses, as the medievalist Marc Bloch pointed out.

Another motive is the quest for the quaint, the lure of antiquarianism. You find this is especially strong in historians of technology, who delight in rediscovering old techniques, mostly for their own sakes. There is an aesthetic delight in learning how to load and fire a black powder gun, but by itself it does not help us understand history. But when we try to imagine Civil War battles and understand the many steps it took to reload one of those things, we come to understand how difficult being a soldier in that period was and simply to marvel when we learn that experienced soldiers could load and fire as fast as three times in a minute. Experience with the artifact does in fact enhance our conception of the past, but it is not anything intrinsic about dealing with the artifact that does so.

Although cost-cutting administrators will always be asking what the point is, there always will be new people turning to the study of the past. As people age, they seek to understand their own place in history, but this may lead them too toward more distant pasts. The skills we develop in finding evidence and analyzing it, especially in the form of texts, and producing analyses in lucid prose of what we have found will serve history students well, whatever medium they may be exploring or writing in.

The history profession in the West is buffeted by many waves, and yet historians continue in their tasks with remarkable clarity of purpose, regardless of the time and place they study. Policy makers do not always turn to us for contexts, but they probably should. We do not know the future, but we have reexperienced the past from close up, and that experience warns us against oversimplification.

The future of the Ancient Near East looks exciting. Digital projects make texts increasingly available through the internet, and being able to search and index collections with computers is in the process of producing interesting new findings. We have not yet seen the fruition of these efforts, but there is no question that we shall. The issue such batches of data pose for the future of the field is the problem both of retrieval and of preservation. As technology advances, it is of vital importance that resources once created remain accessible and can be manipulated in the future without destroying the integrity established for texts by the ancients.

Perhaps it is premature to worry about preservation, but I personally have experienced the elusiveness of data and the loss of data. However enticing digitization is, and however secure it seems, we do all need backup. Books will never die off, in spite of what pundits say. They have covers and can be protected; you can look in their indices and find things. But, yes, they crystallize matters at a given time and place and show the future how little we knew when we put them together. They testify to our current ignorance, but they will last a few hundred years. The Mesopotamians and Egyptians had the right ideas when it came to perpetuating what they wrote; clay and stone will last.

In archaeology also technology will make imaging easier, and x-rays will even now allow penetration of ruins created by humans without the usual destruction of some of the evidence. These techniques will lead to reconstructions of sites in much more detail than is now possible.

But where will the money for such efforts come from? The countries of the region, beset with profound social problems, are hardly likely to spend a whole lot more on the Ancient Near East except perhaps where tourism recommends such expenditures, meaning in Egypt. But such spending may concentrate on making difficult but interesting places accessible, not on finding out new things, especially if they are not visually stunning.

For money for the foreseeable future we must continue to look to the universities in the West and to the meager government funding sources that encourage the human sciences. And that means that the people who can afford seriously to study the Ancient Near East will continue to be few in number, however intrepid and creative they may be.

History today is in trouble, just as many other areas of endeavor are in trouble. But the history of the Ancient Near East teaches us that it is possible, in spite of floods, famines, foreign invasions, and religious change, to muddle through. States may fall, governments may change, and generals fade away. But the common sense and kindness of the peoples of the Ancient Near East persist down to our own time.

GLOSSARY

Abbé: French for "abbot," head of a monastery

Abu Simbel: Modern name for the temple complex Ramses II built 250 km or about 150 miles to the southeast of Elephantine Island

Akhenaten: Egyptian king 1352–1335 BCE who reformed religion by closing down temples to gods other than his favorite, Aten

Akkad: Sargon's capital city, located in central Iraq, from 2300 BCE

Akkadian: Semitic language of Mesopotamia written in cuneiform

Alexander the Great: Macedonian leader 356–323 BCE who conquered the Persian empire

Alexandria: Egyptian port city founded by Alexander the Great and since an important hub of trade

Alphabet: Writing system that expresses each sound that is significant in a language with a separate sign

Amarna Age: The period of religious reform begun by Akhenaten, 1352–1298 BCE

Amunhotep II: 1427–1400 BCE, Egyptian king of the New Kingdom married to Hatshepsut

Amorites: "Westerners" coming into Mesopotamia in the late third millennium BCE, the rulers of most of the states of the early second millennium BCE

Amun: "The Hidden One," chief god of Egypt with an important temple at Thebes

Anatolia: Modern Turkey, "sunrise land" in Greek

Animism: Idea that all natural objects are inhabited by spirits that might affect humans

Aramaic: Semitic language spoken in the Near East in the first millennium BCE

Assur: Capital city of Assyria in northern Iraq

Assyria: State formed on rainfall agriculture land in northern Iraq

Assyriologist: Student of cuneiform culture, so called because Assyria was the first part of that culture discovered

Astrology: Predicting human events on the basis of the movements of the stars and planets

Aswan: City at the first waterfall up the Nile, in many periods the southern limit of the Egyptian state

Aten: Disk of the sun, worshipped almost as the sole god by Akhenaten

Babylon: City of central Iraq, after Hammurapi 1792–1750 BCE, capital of Mesopotamia

Babylonians: People from the city of Mesopotamian Babylon and more generally southern Iraq

BCE: "Before the Common Era" = Before Christ, used in preference to BC because this era has come into worldwide use

Besitun: Mountain in Iran with a trilingual carving put there by the Persian King Darius reigning 521–486 BCE

Canaanites: "Lowlanders" people who lived in Israel before the Israelites arrived about 1200 BCE

CE: The Common Era, the same as the Christian era, beginning with the birth of Christ in 1 CE

Central Asia: The region to the north and east of the Ancient Near East

Chaldees, Chaldeans: Aramaic-speaking tribes who came to dominate far southern Mesopotamia in the middle of the first millennium BCE

Coffin Texts: Spells which Egyptians wrote on coffins praying to allow the dead to reach a happy afterlife

Coptic: Late Egyptian written in an expanded Greek script, the liturgical language of Egyptian Christians

Cuneiform: "Nail-formed" writing developed in Mesopotamia for writing on clay

Cylinder seals: Small tubes with art and sometimes inscriptions on them which were rolled over clay tablets as someone's signature attesting to a document

Cyrus II: Persian emperor ruling 538–530 BCE who conquered Mesopotamia and most of the rest of the Ancient Near East

Demotic: A cursive form of late Egyptian writing developed around 600 BCE

Determinatives: Signs in both Egyptian and in the cuneiform languages that show the reader the category of thing to which the word belongs

Early Dynastic Egypt: Dynasties 0 through 2, from about 3100 to 2680 BCE, in which Egypt was unified under one king

Early Dynastic Mesopotamia: 3100–2300 BCE, a period of competing city states

Elamites: People from western Iran who wrote their language in cuneiform, a language not related to any other

Electrum: Naturally occurring alloy of silver and gold found in Turkey, used for the first coins

Elephantine Island: Spit of land at the first waterfall on the Nile going upstream, which served as a guard post against southerners

Empire: A state that tries to rule other political groups not directly related to its dominant group

Enki: The Mesopotamian god of fresh water and of wisdom

Enlil: The god of Nippur and the chief god of the Mesopotamians

Ethnic states: Tribally based states of the first millennium BCE especially that formed on the basis of previous affiliations of the people involved, depicted as related by family

Etymology: The origins of a word or earliest form of it

Euphrates: The southern river of Mesopotamia running from Turkey through Syria and Iraq, a slow-moving meandering stream

Fars: Southeastern province of Iran

First millennium: The thousand years from 999 BCE to the year 1 BCE

Gaza Strip: Land on the Mediterranean coast between Egypt and Israel

Gilgamesh Epic: Long poem known from 700 BCE going back to early stories around 1700 BCE about a legendary Mesopotamian king who may have lived around 2700 BCE

Greek: Indo-European language spoken in Greece and spread by Alexander's conquests

Gulf of Aqaba: Arm of water stretching north from the Indian Ocean toward Jordan and Israel

Hammurapi: King of Babylon who formed an empire in central Mesopotamia and wrote a monumental law collection, 1792–1750 BCE

Hatshepsut: Egyptian queen who ruled as king while her deceased husband's heir was a minor, reigning 1472–1457 BCE

Hattic: Language spoken in Turkey before the Hittites came, not related to any other

Hattusili III: King of the Hittites who wrote an apology for taking the throne from his nephew and concluded a treaty with Egypt, reigning 1267–1237 BCE

Hebrew Bible: The Bible in Hebrew and Aramaic language that became the Christian Old Testament

Hellenism: The feeling that Greek language and culture should be adopted even by people who did not speak Greek

Henotheism: Idea that there may be many gods, but only one is relevant to a particular group of people

Herodotus: Greek historian who visited Egypt, reporting on other eastern areas before 430 BCE

Hittite: Language and people of central Turkey known from 1700 BCE into the first millennium

Horus: Egyptian falcon god identified with the living king

Hurrian: A language unrelated to any other found in northern Mesopotamia written in cuneiform from 2300 to 1200 BCE

Hyksos: Invaders of Egypt from Asia whose dynasties are the Second Intermediate Period, 1650–1550 BCE

Iliad: Greek poem from about 700 BCE recounting a war between Greeks and Asiatics around 1200 BCE

Indus River: In Pakistan, a center for a complex urban civilization around 2600–1700 BCE

Ionia: Term for the west coast of modern Turkey, in ancient times populated by Greek speakers

Islam: Religion of "Submission" to the One God, formulated by the Prophet Muhammad around 622 CE in central Arabia

Israel: The hill country in the interior of the modern state of Israel where Israelites began forming a state around 1100 BCE

Joshua: Israelite leader and book in the Hebrew Bible detailing the conquest of the land around 1200 BCE

Judahites: People from Judah, the largest tribe in southern Israel; after the split around 925 BCE refers to people of the southern kingdom

Judges: Israelite leaders and book detailing the disorganized responses to outside threats around 1100 BCE

Karnak: Modern name for the enormous Amun temple north of Thebes in Egypt

Kassites: Rulers of Mesopotamia speaking a language unrelated to any other presiding over the longest and most peaceful period of Mesopotamian history, 1500–1200 BCE

Larsa: Southern Mesopotamian city which dominated others in the Early Old Babylonian period, 2000–1800 BCE

List science: Mesopotamian idea that listing all instances of a phenomenon is all the knowledge you need about it

Logogram: Sign that stands for a whole word, like our $

Maat: Egyptian "justice" or "balance," a key value for ancient Egyptians

Maccabean: Referring to Judahite leaders and later kings who won independence from the Seleucids, 164–63 BCE

Macedonia: Northern Greece from which Alexander the Great conquered the known world

Marduk: Chief god of Babylon who was promoted in the Creation Epic to be chief god of Mesopotamia

Mari: City on the middle Euphrates, now just inside Syria, which was an important trading center in the early second millennium BCE

Middle Kingdom: Egypt's Dynasties Eleven through Fourteen between 2055–1650 BCE

Monumentalism: Style of building really big things for religious and political purposes

Moses: Israelite religious leader around 1200 BCE who led Israelites from Egypt into Israel

Mursili II: Hittite king reigning 1321–1295 BCE known for his Plague Prayers

Nabonidus: Last native-born king of Babylonia, reigning 555–539 BCE

Naram-Sin: King of Akkad, grandson of Sargon, reigning 2254–2218 BCE

Naturalism: Artistic idea that artists should try to make their creations resemble the people or things depicted

Neo-Babylonian: Dynasty ruling the southern half of the Near East 605–539 BCE while the Persians ruled the north

New Kingdom: Dynasties Eighteen and Nineteen in Egypt, 1550–1069 BCE, also known as the Empire Period

Nile Delta: The river-created plain north of modern Cairo where the river meanders toward the Mediterranean

Nineveh: Capital of the Neo-Assyrian empire in northern Iraq

Nippur: Religious capital of Sumer in southern Iraq

Noah: Israelite flood hero in the Hebrew Bible

Nomads: People who follow livestock through the seasons looking for pasture

Northern Tier: The northernmost countries of the modern Middle East, including Turkey, Iraq, and Iran

Nubia: The Nile Valley south of Aswan, encompassed by the modern country of Sudan; an independent but Egyptian-influenced kingdom in the first millennium BCE

Old Kingdom: Egypt's Dynasties Three to Six, 2663–2160 BCE

Omen: Sign to predict the future ranging from sheep livers to oil on water to star-gazing

Orient: The East, the term Europeans used before World War I for the whole of Asia

Oriental despotism: Idea that oppressive eastern regimes arose because of the need to build and regulate irrigation systems

Orientalism: Idea that Westerners who study the East do so in order to conquer and rule it

Orontes River: The main river in Lebanon, central Syria, and Turkey, the modern al-Asi

Osiris, *Wsyr* : Egyptian god of the dead, identified with the deceased father of the present king

Palestine: The coast of Israel around Gaza, named after the Philistines, but by extension the country behind Gaza

Palmyrenes: People living in Palmyra, an oasis in the Syrian desert, who wrote in Aramaic in the late first millennium BCE and early first millennium CE

Pantheon: All the gods of a culture considered as a whole

Parthians: Zoroastrian dynasty that ruled the East including Iraq from 250 BCE to 226 CE

Persepolis: Capital of Persians in central Iran

Philologist: Scholar concerned with words in their cultural contexts

Phoenician: Person from the Syrian and Lebanese coast in the first millennium BCE

Polytheism: View that there are many gods with different powers and personalities

Ptolemies: Greek-speaking kings of Egypt after Alexander, 323–30 BCE

Ptolemy: Egyptian scholar of the early first millennium CE who formulated a view of the solar system with the earth at the center

Pythagorean Theorem: Geometrical idea that the sum of the squares of the sides of a right triangle are equal to the square of its hypotenuse

Ramses II: Longest-lived New Kingdom Egyptian ruler 1279–1212 BCE who built many monuments

Relief sculpture: Stone carving with features either indented into or protruding from the surface

Rosetta Stone: Egyptian trilingual decree dated 196 BCE, discovered near the western mouth of the Nile and a key element in the decipherment of hieroglyphics

Sargon: Founding king of the Old Akkadian empire, reigning 2334–2279 BCE

Sargon II: Assyrian king reigning 721–705 BCE

Sassanian: Iranian Zoroastrian dynasty ruling Mesopotamia and Iran 224–651 CE

Saul: First king of Israel, around 1040 BCE

Sea Peoples: Peoples of the Aegean who invaded the Near East around 1200 BCE

Second Isaiah: Jewish prophet living in Babylonian exile around 539 BCE whose writings were joined to those of the earlier prophet Isaiah, now chapters 40–55 of that Book

Second millennium: Period from 1999 to 1000 BCE

Seleucids: Greek kings after Alexander who ruled Syria and Iraq, 305–95 BCE

Sexagesimal: Relating to the number system on base sixty, so that $1,0 = 60$, the basic Mesopotamian system

Sub-Saharan Africa: Africa below the desert

Sumer: Southern Iraq south of modern Baghdad

Sumerian: Language of southern Iraqis in the most ancient times, not related to any other

Syllabary: A writing system that records syllables, like /ka/ and /ak/ or /kak/, but not individual sounds

Syria: Western Mesopotamia including the modern state of Syria

Thebes: Greek name for the city in central Egypt from which many kings came

Third millennium: Period from 2999 to 2000 BCE

Thutmosis III: Empire-building New Kingdom Egyptian king, reigning 1479–1424 BCE

Tigris: Easternmost river of Mesopotamia, in some places rapidly flowing with steep cliffs

Trilingual: Inscription with three languages used to convey the same message

Tutankhamun, Tut: Son and heir 1335–1325 BCE of the Egyptian king Akhenaten, whose small but glorious tomb was found almost intact

Ugaritic: Language and writing system from the Syrian coast in the late second millennium which experimented with simplified consonantal writing

Ur: Southernmost large city in Mesopotamia, a seaport city

Yahweh: Personal name of the God of Israel, probably meaning "He causes to be"

Zagros: Mountains in eastern Iraq which in some periods formed the border with Iran

Ziggurat: Temple tower built of solid mud brick in Mesopotamia

Zoroaster, Zoroastrianism: A prophet and his religion, founded between 1000 and 500 BCE, stressing the idea that there is a good god who is constantly fighting with a bad god, and humans must obey the good god

FURTHER READING

Here are some helpful works that students might want to look into next to deepen their understanding of the Ancient Near East. We categorize them as follows: Bibliographies, Encyclopedias, Anthologies of ancient texts, and Stimulating studies. We will concentrate on works in English, hoping that those who read other languages will be able to find equivalent resources through references in the English works.

BIBLIOGRAPHIES

The bibliography of work on cuneiform is now online, called *Keilschriftbibliographie* at < vergil.uni-tuebingen.de/keibi/ >; previously it was published in the journal *Orientalia*. For Egyptian there are several websites that attempt to keep up with the bibliography in that field. Hebrew Bible too has the *Elenchus of Biblica* now migrating online for the history of ancient Israel but including many other related areas.

ENCYCLOPEDIAS

Jack Sasson's four-volume *Civilizations of the Ancient Near East,* New York: Scribner's, 1992, is a helpful place to start, and it has a great index. And for Israel don't forget the many dictionaries of the Bible, especially Katharine Doob Sakenfeld, editor, *New Interpreter's Dictionary of the Bible*, Nashville, TN: Abingdon, 2006, and online *The Catholic Encyclopedia*. More technical, but not all in German, is the still incomplete *Reallexikon der Assyriologie,* Berlin: de Gruyter, 1928-, and the *Lexicon der Aegyptologie,* Wiesbaden: Harrassowitz, 1972–92. For archaeology Eric Meyers' *The Oxford Encyclopedia of Archaeology in the Near East,* New York: Oxford University Press, 1997, is helpful and has articles ranging more broadly than its title might indicate. My *A Companion to the Ancient Near East,* Malden, MA: Blackwell, 2005, has articles on many topics, as do the *Oxford Companion to Ancient Anatolia,* edited by Sharon Steadman and Gregory McMahon, Oxford: Oxford University Press, 2011, and the *Oxford Companion to Cuneiform Cultures,* edited by Karen Radner and Eleanor Robson, Oxford: Oxford University Press, 2011.

ANTHOLOGIES

The old standby is James Pritchard's *Ancient Near Eastern Texts,* Princeton, NJ: Princeton University Press, 1969, which still has a wider range of translations than more recent anthologies. A competitor might be the three-volume *The Context of Scripture,* edited by W. W. Hallo and K. Lawson Younger, Jr., but it is very expensive, Leiden: Brill, 1997, 2000, 2002. Benjamin Foster's *Before the Muses: An Anthology of Akkadian Literature,* Bethesda, MD: CDL, 2005, translates the memorable pieces of literature in Akkadian only, and Jeremy Black's *The Literature of Ancient Sumer,* Oxford: Oxford University Press, 2004, does the same for Sumerian. For Egyptian William Kelly Simpson's *Literature of Ancient Egypt,* New Haven, CT: Yale, 2003, translates the major pieces, and Miriam Lichtheim's three-volume collection *Ancient Egyptian Literature,* Los Angeles, CA: University of California Press, 1975, 1976, 1980, is worth consulting. The Society of Biblical Literature has an active list of small volumes of translations of texts from particular periods which can be very helpful. Mark Chavalas, editor, *The Ancient Near East: Historical Sources in Translation,* Malden, MA: Blackwell, 2006, and his colla- borators have translated the Mesopotamian royal inscriptions from many periods. Online resources include the CDLI, < cdli.ucla.edu >, the Cuneiform Data Library Information site run by the University of California at Los Angeles for economic texts, and Oxford's Sumerian Literature Project, < etcsl.orinst.ox.ac.uk >; the sites are frequently updated and so can give the most recent insights in translation.

STIMULATING STUDIES

Difficult but still worth reading is A. Leo Oppenheim's *Ancient Mesopotamia,* Chicago, IL: University of Chicago Press, 1964, an opinionated and erudite introduction. I have found John Wilson's eloquent *The Culture of Ancient*

Egypt, Chicago, IL: University of Chicago Press, 1951, to be helpful. For religion for both of the major cultures Henri Frankfort's *Kingship and the Gods* is very clear, Chicago, IL: University of Chicago Press, 1948. From later times Wolfram von Soden's *The Ancient Orient,* Grand Rapids, MI: Eerdmans, 1994; German: 1992, sums up the views of the leading Assyriologist of Germany. I have found the various studies of Jan Assmann to be very engaging, especially his intellectual history of Egypt, translated as *The Mind of Egypt,* New York: Metropolitan, 2002, German: 1996.

Among textbook introductions Ian Shaw's *Oxford History of Ancient Egypt,* Oxford: Oxford University Press, 2000, is both beautiful and well informed. More recent is Salima Ikram's *Ancient Egypt,* Cambridge: Cambridge University Press, 2010, with her own marvelous pictures from her scampering all over the country. Some people have found my 1997 *Life in the Ancient Near East,* New Haven, CT and London: Yale University Press, to be a helpful beginning at understanding social and economic life. It is too early to say if the same will be said of my 2011 book *Religions of the Ancient Near East,* Cambridge: Cambridge University Press.

On Egyptian art still interesting is H. A. Groenewegen-Frankfort, *Arrest and Movement: Space and Time in the Art of the Ancient Near East,* Cambridge, MA: Harvard University Press, 1951, 1987. D. Snell, in Sasson 1992, recapitulates the arguments about coins. Daniel Fleming, *Democracy's Ancient Ancestors: Mari and Early Collective Governance,* Cambridge: Cambridge University Press, 2004, brings together the evidence for governing councils. H. W. F. Saggs, *Encounter With the Divine in Mesopotamia and Israel,* London: Athlone, 1978, is a ground-breaking comparison sympathetic to both elements. Peter Daniels has described what you need for decipherment, "'Shewing of Hard Sentences and Dissolving of Doubts': The First Decipherment," *Journal of the American Oriental Society* 108, 1988, pages 419–36, and compare his valuable study on Edward Hincks in *The Edward Hincks Bicentenary Lectures,* Dublin: University College, 1994, pages 30–57.

On the contrast between the French and the English ways of publicizing their discoveries see Friedrich N. Bohrer, "Inventing Assyria: Exoticism and Reception in Nineteenth-century England and France," *The Art Bulletin* 80, 1998, pages 336–56. The reference to the House of David is in the Inscription from Tell Dan in northern Israel, A. Biran and J. Naveh, "An Aramaic Stele Fragment from Tel Dan," *Israel Exploration Journal* 43, 1993, pages 81–98; in general see Hershel Shanks, editor, *Ancient Israel,* Boston, MA: Prentice Hall and Washington, DC: Biblical Archaeological Society, 2011. Benno Landsberger's 1926 essay was translated by Benjamin Foster, "The Conceptual Autonomy of the Mesopotamian World," Malibu, CA: Undena, 1976. On deciphering Egyptian see Lesley and Roy Adkins, *The Keys of Egypt: The Obsession to Decipher Egyptian Hieroglyphics,* New York:

HarperCollins, 2000. On modern Egyptian study of ancient Egypt, see Donald Malcolm Reid, *Whose Pharaohs? Archaeology, Museums, and Egyptian National Identity from Napoleon to World War I,* Berkeley, CA: University of California Press, 2002. Trevor Bryce, *The Kingdom of the Hittites,* Oxford: Oxford University Press, 1998, sketches the political history. For birth rituals see Gary Beckman, *Hittite Birth Rituals,* Wiesbaden: Harrassowitz, 1983.

For Johan Huizinga's definition of history see his essay, in R. Klibansky and H. J. Paton, editors, *Philosophy and History,* New York: Harper, 1963, first published: 1936, pages 1–10. Marc Bloch explored the myth of origins in his *The Historian's Craft,* New York: Vintage, 1953.

INDEX

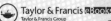